REVIEWS OF THE STAGE PRODUCTIONS

Letters from Battle River:
"Engaging and enthralling . . . a love letter to this part of the world, and it connects you to the cultural and geographic uniqueness of Alberta that those of us who live here can easily take for granted." —*See Magazine*

"A delightful trip into recent history . . . through the eyes of a remarkable Alberta woman . . . The closest one could come to experiencing, touching, tasting how life would have been, just 80 years ago in this area." —*Edmonton Sun*

Respecting the Action for Seduction:
"Wears its history lightly, a great feat." —*Edmonton Journal*

"Fans of historical drama, *A&E* or *The History Channel* will be overjoyed." —*Edmonton Sun*

The Unmarried Wife:
"A fascinating story about the love between photographer Ernest Brown and his assistant, Gladys Reeves. The script is clever." —*Global Television*

"Thoughtfully written scenes . . . create a stirring though compacted narrative amongst the lineage." —*Vue Weekly*

"The tacit understanding that eccentricity and passion, illicit or otherwise, are inimical to Alberta history gets exploded in the course of this intriguing little show." —*Edmonton Journal*

Firing Lines:
"The stories themselves are intriguing . . . Offer[s] us a chance to see history questioned instead of merely presented." —*Vue Weekly*

"A workmanlike production that introduces us to a fascinating and little known Canadian journalist . . . Dramatic and often heartbreaking stories of life in wartime." —*Edmonton Sun*

"Completely riveting . . . Playwright Debbie Marshall has telescoped 20 of Nasmyth's wartime letters into a drama that tugs at every emotion." —*St. Albert Gazette*

HER VOICE, HER CENTURY

HER VOICE,

HER CENTURY

FOUR PLAYS ABOUT DARING WOMEN

David Cheoros, Karen Simonson, and Debbie Marshall

BRINDLE
& GLASS

Brindle & Glass Publishing Ltd.
brindleandglass.com

LIBRARY AND ARCHIVES CANADA CATALOGUING IN PUBLICATION
Cheoros David, 1969–
Her voice, her century : four plays about daring
women / David Cheoros, Karen Simonson, Debbie Marshall.

Contents: Letters from battle river / David Cheoros and Karen
Simonson — Respecting the action for seduction / David
Cheoros and Karen Simonson — The unmarried wife / David
Cheoros and Karen Simonson — Firing lines / Debbie Marshall.
Issued also in electronic format.
ISBN 978-1-926972-99-2

1. Canadian drama (English)—21st century. 2. Historical drama,
Canadian (English). 3. Women—Canada, Western—Drama. 4. Canada,
Western—Drama. I. Marshall, Debbie, 1959– II. Simonson, Karen, 1978–
III. Title. IV. Title: Four plays about daring women.

PS8309.W6C44 2012   C812'.60803522   C2012-902604-2

Proofreader: Lenore Hietkamp
Cover photo: *Women Hunting in the Rockies*, Provincial Archives of Alberta, A3939
Design: Pete Kohut

Brindle & Glass is pleased to acknowledge the financial support for its publishing
program from the Government of Canada through the Canada Book Fund, Canada
Council for the Arts, and the Province of British Columbia through the British
Columbia Arts Council and the Book Publishing Tax Credit.

The interior pages of this book have been printed on 100% post-consumer
recycled paper, processed chlorine free, and printed with vegetable-based inks.

1 2 3 4 5 16 15 14 13 12

PRINTED IN CANADA

To archivists everywhere, and the researchers who love them.

CONTENTS

FOREWORD

Archives hold a treasure trove of stories, many of which rarely see the light of day. The majority of archival researchers are genealogists, coming to archives mainly to explore the records that can help fill in their family trees. Academics primarily come to archives with a topic already in mind, hoping to find records to explore and support their research.

It is rare for researchers to come to archives with an open mind, letting the records guide and inspire their work process. This approach is more difficult, as most people need to have a place to start. This is where archivists can be extremely helpful. They have knowledge of the archival holdings that cannot be compared to even the best finding aid. They know some of the gems in the holdings. By engaging artists in the content available in archival holdings, archivists could become charged with the responsibility of disseminating and interpreting the stories archives preserve. MAA and PAA Theatre has dramatized records that are not often viewed by researchers. In the process, they have promoted the Provincial Archives of Alberta and its holdings, and shown Albertans their own history.

It has been the pleasure of the Provincial Archives to support the development of all the plays contained in this volume. More and more people are finding innovative ways to use archives, especially as online tools and better databases make the Archives' resources more completely open and accessible to everyone. After almost twenty years with the Archives, I still marvel at the creativity that a really good story can unleash. Our collaboration with MAA and PAA Theatre has provided the Archives with an interesting and unique way to transform our image from a sealed vault to a window on our past.

Enjoy!

—Irene Jendzjowsky
Director Emeritus
Provincial Archives of Alberta

INTRODUCTION

For the three years before I became a reference archivist at the Provincial Archives of Alberta (PAA), I worked at the Archives on contract. My job involved writing descriptions for the government and private records held by the PAA. I saw many documents that no one had touched since they'd been acquired, sometimes for decades. As I learned about the fascinating lives of these individuals, I wanted to explore fresh new ways to share their stories with others. In 2006, I got an opportunity to do so.

That year, the PAA organized its first "Voices of the Past," an event in which original archival records were read aloud to an audience. These included several letters by Dr. Mary Percy Jackson, a pioneer physician in northern Alberta in the 1920s. I was at the event as part of my work at the PAA. My husband, David Cheoros, then general manager of Theatre Network and former director of the Edmonton International Fringe Festival, was volunteering that night to read a different selection of records. Our good friend Heather Swain, an actor and performer, was also present.

As we drove home afterward, it was thrilling to hear David and Heather—neither of whom had ever done research in an archives—chatting enthusiastically about Jackson's correspondence. Both felt that her letters were quite theatrical and would make an excellent Fringe play. David and I eventually decided to make that dream a reality, setting in motion the steps that would lead to our first production, *Letters from Battle River: The Adventures of Dr. Mary Percy Jackson*. It wouldn't be easy.

The PAA had received the records in the Mary Percy Jackson fonds in three accessions between 1994 and 2001. There is just over one metre of textual records as well as four audio cassettes. The fonds primarily consists of correspondence between Mary Percy Jackson and her friends and family in Canada and England. Luckily for us, through the efforts of the PAA and the Archives Society of Alberta, Mary Percy Jackson's early letters had been digitized, and were available online.

David spent countless hours transcribing these letters into a Word document in order to make them more manageable for us to work with.

Two years' worth of letters is a lot of letters and a lot of fabulous content, too much for an hour-long show. Since we couldn't include every letter, David and I read through them, selecting our favourites. Eventually, we made our final choices and crafted *Letters from Battle River*. Our new production company—MAA and PAA Theatre, specializing in historical plays with contemporary relevance—would launch the play at the 2007 Edmonton International Fringe Festival.

As we worked together, David and I learned that we brought very different things to the playwriting process. David is a theatre guy, and is always concerned about the narrative, about creating a kind of story arc. As an historian, I don't mind if the bits of the story occasionally fit together oddly. What's important is to be accurate, to represent the words and thoughts of our subjects and their time periods. I want to be dispassionate, David passionate. Both qualities would be vitally important for the next two shows we would do together.

At first, it was hard to decide what story to explore for our second play. There are a lot of records at the PAA! After some initial research without much inspiration, Director of Access and Preservation Services Irene Jendzjowsky suggested the scandalous affair between former Premier John Brownlee and Vivian MacMillan. The newspapers of the 1930s had reported extensively on the resulting court case, with detailed transcripts of the trial. The PAA also held the court case file, with a transcript of the court case. We also uncovered surprising information, such as MacMillan's name in a divorce file (she was named as having an affair with a man who later became her husband). Some research is like following a line of bread crumbs.

Flipping through these files, David and I learned that what actually happened between those two people will likely always be a mystery, as both provided widely differing accounts of what happened—MacMillan claiming seduction, and Brownlee no affair at all. We decided to leave it up to our audience to determine the truth. In *Respecting the Action for Seduction*, we used dramatizations and recreations of trial scenes, presenting the claims of both Brownlee and MacMillan. Then we speculated on a third option, something more "middle of the road."

For our third play, we focused on the records of Ernest Brown and Gladys Reeves, two early Edmonton photographers. Nothing in the available biographical information recorded an affair between them (Brown was already married), but letters in their fonds clearly suggested that an affair did happen. For *The Unmarried Wife: The Passion and Photography of Gladys Reeves and Ernest Brown*, we used a combination of verbatim letters and dramatized scenes to present an alternative story of their lives and love. Juicy tidbits took on new significance for the play. For instance, in her will, Brown's wife mentioned that Gladys was in possession of a desk that belonged to her husband. Why was that so important to her? We will never really know, but it makes for some interesting speculation.

Part of the trick in writing historical plays is in finding the right set of records to use. Most of the time, the PAA doesn't receive complete records created over the course of the entire life of an individual. There might be a scattering of letters and other documents, sometimes enough to construct a story, sometimes not. This can make finding the right records difficult. One of the priorities that MAA and PAA Theatre has maintained is the frequent use of verbatim records. We thought it was important to have our subjects' own words well represented. But of course, records don't necessarily tell the whole story. Not everyone wants every aspect of their life open to researchers in the archives. Inevitably this leaves gaps, which we may fill in, based on the existing records and our understanding of the people with whom we are dealing.

Karen Simonson and David Cheoros.

In 2011, knowing that both of us would be caught up in another production—our daughter Sophia, who would be born mid-Fringe Festival—we invited author Debbie Marshall to write a play for MAA and PAA Theatre. Debbie had earlier written a biography of Roberta MacAdams, one of the first female MLAs in Alberta. She had an idea for a play about Beatrice Nasmyth, MacAdams's campaign manager. Nasmyth had been a reporter in England during the First World War. In addition to reporting for the *Vancouver Province*, Nasmyth had also worked in the London office of the Alberta Agent General.

Debbie's play—*Firing Lines*—diverged from our previous plays because it was not primarily based on records held by the PAA. The records she used were still in the hands of Nasmyth's descendants, though this did dovetail with the PAA's outreach activities on how to maintain your own family records. However, Nasmyth was an Alberta government employee and there were orders-in-council at the PAA related to her employment as a civil servant. She was also the second cousin of Alberta Premier Arthur Sifton and his brother Clifford Sifton, the architect of early prairie settlement. Accordingly, many of the articles she filed reflected her Alberta connections. For instance, Nasmyth often described the contributions and sacrifice of many Albertans who fought during the Great War. These stories and many others found their way into *Firing Lines*.

Already, we have a wish list of subjects to keep us busy for the next five years. I am looking forward to diving into another set of records, digging around in them for a while until the shape of another exciting new story appears.

—Karen Simonson
Reference Archivist at the PAA

Mary Percy Jackson had thought herself prepared for frontier riding, but was shocked to discover that English side-saddle riding bore little resemblance to riding through the northern Alberta brush in the middle of the night.
FAMILY COLLECTION

LETTERS FROM BATTLE RIVER

THE ADVENTURES OF
DR. MARY PERCY JACKSON

ADAPTED FOR THE STAGE BY
DAVID CHEOROS AND KAREN SIMONSON

Heather D. Swain, with a projection of Mary Percy Jackson.
IAN JACKSON/EPIC PHOTOGRAPHY

Mary Percy Jackson with Lesley Ann and John Robert Jackson.
PROVINCIAL ARCHIVES OF ALBERTA, PRI970.0342/2, PHOTO 51

MARY PERCY JACKSON

Mary Percy was born on December 27, 1904, in Dudley, England (Dudley is just outside Birmingham). In 1927, she graduated from the University of Birmingham with a bachelor of surgery and bachelor of medicine. She then worked for a time at the Birmingham General Hospital. Eager for adventure, Mary intended to go and practise medicine in India. However, those placements came up only every two years. While waiting for the India placement, she read an advertisement in the *British Medical Journal* for women doctors to practise in Alberta. Mary applied and left for Canada, intending to spend only one year there. She was sent by the Alberta government's district medical officer to the Battle River district, in the northern part of the Peace River country in northern Alberta.

On March 10, 1931, she married widower Frank Jackson, an English-born fur-trader and farmer with three sons, Louis Albert, Arthur Carl, and Frank Jr. Frank's first wife, Louise Barr, had died shortly after giving birth to their third son. Frank and Mary had two children, Lesley Anne and John Robert. She left Battle River when she married, and gave up her contract with the government. She moved further north, to Keg River, where Frank had been living for many years. At Keg River, the nearest doctors were one hundred and twenty-five miles south, at Peace River, and one hundred and twenty-five miles northeast, at Fort Vermillion, both of which were inaccessible most of the time.

As a married woman, Mary could no longer practise medicine for the Alberta government. Nevertheless, she did continue to practise, in an office and waiting room Frank built for her in the basement of their house. She practised extensively among the Metis population in the area, which she found extremely satisfying. Mary retired in 1974, when Frank became ill. He died in 1979.

Mary was a woman who had earned many accolades. In 1975, she was named "Woman of the Year" by the *Voice of Native Women*; in 1976, she was presented an honorary doctor of laws degree from the University of Alberta; in 1983, she was named to the Alberta Order of Excellence; and in 1989, she was appointed to the Order of Canada.

A heroic example of the pioneer spirit and commitment of northern doctors, she devoted her life to ministering to the Indians, Metis and immigrants of northwestern Alberta. Undaunted by the expansiveness of her territory, the receipt of payment in barter, the primitive transportation or the inadequate medical facilities and equipment, she has served Canadians with great dedication, skill and sacrifice. (Order of Canada)

Mary resided in Keg River until moving to Manning around 1996. She died May 6, 2000.

My last letter to you only left yesterday, and here I am writing again. I hope you won't get tired of my effusions. Really, if I wrote all I wanted, you'd be getting about twenty pages a day! I hope you'll keep my letters. I should rather like to have them myself in my old age. They take the place of a diary! I meant to keep a diary, but soon discovered that life was too short to write down all interesting things that happened. I am trying to tell you about things as soon as they happen, because I'm already getting so used to things that I can hardly realize how different they will all seem to you. (Mary Percy Jackson, August 4, 1929)

Mary wrote letters regularly to friends and family. She wrote hundreds of letters to those back in England, most frequently in 1929, a little less often in 1930, and then sporadically in 1931 just before her marriage to Frank Jackson in March. In *Letters from Battle River*, we were unable to use all of Mary's letters (there were just too many!). The sequence of the letters was also altered, and contents from several letters were sometimes combined into a single section. We kept the letters' original language—some of which today may be offensive, but was nevertheless common at the time.

To read Mary's letters in their entirety, visit the Provincial Archives of Alberta. To view her letters online, visit the Archives Society of Alberta's "In Word" database. The letters have also appeared in book form. They were originally written to a number of individuals and were circulated among friends in England. In 1933, these were collected and published as *On the Last Frontier: Pioneering in the Peace River Block: Letters of Mary Percy Jackson*. This book is available in the Provincial Archives of Alberta's reference library. The letters were also edited by Janice Dickin and published in 1996, in a collection entitled *Suitable for the Wilds*.

This play is a one-woman show. All lines are read by "Mary Percy Jackson" (**MPJ**).

SET

The set is *very* simple—either a writing desk and chair, or perhaps nothing at all. The performance is accompanied by items of the period and many still images of individuals and locations (ours were from the Provincial Archives of Alberta). Mary Percy Jackson sometimes sees and interacts with these objects and images.

The original production was performed on a bare stage approximately eight feet square.

COSTUMES

Costuming is simple—a tight-fitting wool jacket and pencil skirt combination that is removed early in the play to reveal pantaloons and a loose cotton shirt.

PRE-SHOW

The following text, made to look like a newspaper ad, is projected onto a wall at the back of the stage:

> Strong Energetic Medical Women with post-graduate experience in Midwifery, wanted for country work in Western Canada, under the Provincial Government Department of Health. The ability to ride a saddle horse would be a great advantage. Apply in first instance to Dr. E.M. Johnstone, c/o Fellowship of the Maple Leaf, 13 Victoria Street, London, SW1.

Scene 1: The Ship

Slide: SS Empress of Scotland—*from brochure.*

MPJ: SS *Empress of Scotland,* about fifty degrees north, forty degrees west, June 12, 1929.

Well we've got over the worst of it now I think, and I'm really enjoying life—but Monday was awful. Very cold, very wet, and very rough.

Slide: ship in rough sea.

The sea was washing over the promenade deck, and even came over the top deck once and soaked my rug! Every now and then, as we went down into a trough, the propeller was right out of water and raced—a horrible sensation. I'd really felt that I'd like the wretched ship to sink! You'll gather from this that I'm not quite as good a sailor as I'd thought!

Slide: smiling white man in '20s suit.

There's a man from Edmonton on board who has told us quite a lot about Alberta. It has a large non-British population apparently—I hope I don't have to practise among Poles or Russians!

Scene 2: Quebec City

Slide: arrival in Quebec.

MPJ: Quebec is a wonderful city—but quite French. The buildings are French. The people talk French. And all the notices and advertisements are in French, sometimes with English underneath. We went right up the hill—there's a lovely view up and down the river. We were dying to go into Château Frontenac—

Slide: Château Frontenac.

—which is an enormous hotel—and demand ice cream, just to see what the inside was like. But we felt that 8:00 AM on a Sunday was not quite the hour to ask for ice cream!

The old castle itself is at the top of the hill—very strongly fortified. Was it the heights of Quebec Wolfe scaled? If so, it must have been jolly hard work.

Scene 3: The Train

Slide: train station.

MPJ: We have just left Port Arthur and Fort William, and expect to reach Winnipeg in nine hours.

Slide: Canadian Shield, repeated under the next few words until it stops being funny.

We have been passing through forest now for thirty-six hours.

Slide: log boom.

There are tree trunks floating down all the rivers. Some of the rivers are side to side with wood. When we were in Ottawa we were shown how the big booms are made, and saw several big paper and pulp factories. But in spite of the millions of tree trunks we've seen about, they don't seem to have made any impression on the forests.

Slide: flat prairie.

We are on the last stage of our journey, and are crossing the prairies toward Saskatoon. These small towns and villages are most amusing. All the inhabitants turn out to see the train.

Slide: woman in pants.

The girls in these western towns wear the same sort of clothes as the men. Shirts, cotton trousers, and braces—a nice cool-looking get-up.

Scene 4: Edmonton

Slide: film clip of train crossing Edmonton's High Level Bridge toward legislature.

MPJ: Edmonton, Alberta, June 20.

I arrived at 7:00 AM and interviewed the deputy minister of health at eleven.

Slide: legislature.

We go in to see the minister himself at two thirty.

Slide: women crossing Jasper Avenue, Edmonton.

Oh it's a funny place, I assure you. Food is much the same—but they've some exciting extras—hot dog, waffles and syrup, and squash pie seem to be favourites. I haven't tasted hot dog yet—it seems to be a sausage between two biscuits.

Slide: Great Dane puppy.

I bought myself a dog yesterday. A pedigree Great Dane! Yes, quite mad, I know, but he's a lovely little pup. Six weeks old. He's being taken to a construction camp to be kept till I am settled down and can take him. His father is an enormous dog. When I was sitting in a chair—he wagged his tail and nearly knocked my glasses off!

Scene 5: The Assignment

MPJ: Thursday, July 4.

Glory hallelujah, and likewise hooroosh. By the time you get this,

Slide: hand-drawn map of Battle River Prairie district.

I hope to be on my way to Battle River Prairie, on the Notikewin River, which is to be my district.

Slide: Notikewin River.

> It's the newest and most exciting district in Alberta. One hundred miles from the nearest town. No telegraph, no telephone.

Slide: small boat on river.

> Mail delivered occasionally by boat up the river. They throw the mail bags out on the bank and there they lie till someone finds them! You must admit, it sounds exciting.

Slide: map that ends at Peace River.

> I don't know whether you'll be able to find it on the *Times Atlas*. It lies west of the Peace River, about eighteen miles, and a hundred miles north of the town called Peace River.

Scene 6: The Arrival In Notikewin

Slide: Peace River train station.

MPJ: The train got in to Peace River at 11:00 AM.

Slide: river boat.

> The boat sailed up the river after 7:00 PM and we eventually landed at 8:30 AM.

Slide: unloading the stuff.

> You should have seen me and my luggage. Twenty-nine pieces weighing over a thousand pounds, and one small wagon to take the lot and Miss Brighty—

Slide: Miss Brighty.

> from the department—and me. With the aid of the captain, the purser, Mr. Lawrence, a parson on his way to Fort Vermilion, two traders on their way north, and some of the crew, we got the wagon loaded and set off—cheered on our way by the entire ship's company, who all got off the boat to wave goodbye!

Mary Percy Jackson and her luggage arrive in Notikewin, July 16, 1929.
Pictured with Sheridan Lawrence and Bon House.
FAMILY COLLECTION

Slide: posing in front of the wagon.

All went well for about half an hour.

Slide: hand-drawn map of the hill.

Then we came to the hill. Miss Brighty and I got off and the horses managed to get about a quarter of the way up and then stuck. There was nothing for it but to unload

Slide: tons of baggage.

and carry the trunks, etc., up the steep bit they'd stuck on. Ninety-five in the shade—mosquitoes by the millions—and you remember the weight of my baggage? We had to do that twice.

Slide: more from wagon.

The man told us it was two miles farther to water—so we plodded on—only to find that the "water" was a filthy little puddle, black with mosquito larvae! However, he assured us that it was the only water between Peace River and Battle River—so we made tea!

Slide: MPJ and Miss Brighty smiling.

I liked the idea of going into a new country with all my goods on a wagon, and me walking behind in true homesteader style, but there are more comfortable ways of travelling.

Scene 7: Unpacking

MPJ: Since our arrival, I've been frightfully busy unpacking the twenty-two boxes and crates of drugs and instruments—cleaning up the house and so on.

Slide: shack in distance.

Mary's original shack in Notikewin (now Manning).
FAMILY COLLECTION

My shack is really topping. I've a big living room, kitchen, a bedroom, and a dispensary-consulting room.

A few yards in front runs a narrow trail, which is the main road north. My house is on the bank of the First Battle River, fifty feet above the stream.

Slide: fording a stream.

The river is very stony and rapid. There is a ford across it, not far from my house. The water comes above hubs of wagon wheels, and I haven't seen a car get across without horses to help it yet. They have just started to build a bridge over the river above the ford.

Slide: bridge with line of people.

So far, they've only got a wooden framework up, but it is possible to get across. It is rather a nightmare in one place as there were only two planks along twenty feet of it—fifty feet above the water, and very springy. That's the way I have to cross. It is quite impossible in a wind. The bridge engineer informed me that they'd put two planks only so that they'd have a chance to help me across. As I'd managed without help, they've added a third plank.

Brutus greets a car crossing the new bridge at Notikewin.
FAMILY COLLECTION

Scene 8: First Dance

MPJ: Friday night, there was a dance in the schoolhouse, four miles away. It was a shriek.

SX: scratchy fiddle or plinky mandolin music.

Slide: exterior of schoolhouse.

> There was just the one big room. You hung your coat and hat on a nail—and powdered your nose in full view of the world. There were crowds more men than women, and half the women were half breeds. The men wore their ordinary clothes—pretty grubby, most of them.

Slide: dancing feet.

> Their boots ranged from hobnailed clogs to riding boots, and galoshes, and moccasins; and you can imagine what my feet felt like by morning.

> There were no programs. In fact, you didn't even have one dance with a man. Every now and then another man would come up behind the one you were dancing with, tap him on the shoulder, and then go off with you! As there were lots more men than women, this happened pretty often!

Slide: musicians.

> The music was one violin and one mandolin, played by Mr. and Mrs. Fife . . . but as she could only play in one key, the tunes were a bit limited!

Scene 9: Starting Work

Slide: MPJ on horseback.

MPJ: I've really been pretty busy these last two or three weeks. I did over one hundred and fifty miles on horseback last week! Really, one needs the strength of an Amazon. If ever there is much sickness about, I shall need help. There's hardly any illness about just now.

I've been seeing mainly accidents and oddments. I've seen five fractures in five weeks!

Slide: girl in foreground, family behind.

The one that has taken up so much time is a little girl of seven. She broke her arm, also dislocated her elbow—a beastly mess. Her brother, aged twelve, came to fetch me. I think he's the bravest kid I've ever met. He had to ride fifteen miles after dark, ford two rivers, and come through a wood in which he'd seen bear tracks to get me. He arrived here at 1:00 AM! We didn't get there till 5:45 AM, as his horse went lame. And the fatherly way he looked after me was delightful.

It was bitterly cold, and he wasn't very warmly clad. He must have been nearly done in when we got there. He insisted that he wasn't tired, though.

Scene 10: VIPs

Slide: Premier on raft.

MPJ: Sunday, August 4.

Oh I had a real day out yesterday. The premier and two MPs and the principal of Alberta University and several other big bugs came out to view the new bridge.

Slide: new bridge with crowd.

They made sundry speeches. All were most frightfully complimentary about me and most of them called on me. Thank heaven I'd finished scrubbing the floor when the first one arrived! I trotted round with them and generally behaved as though I was used to the society of prime ministers. The locals looked most impressed!

Slide: town of Frank nearly concealed by wheat.

I gather that this district has the finest wheat crop in Alberta this year—and it's certainly lovely to look on. Mr. Schamehorn is the owner of the finest crop round here, and he says he can hardly sleep at night for fear something will happen before he gets it harvested. He's been out here eighteen months, and of course this crop means everything to him. That is the snag about homesteading—you can't get a penny out of the land in less than two years, and if anything happens to that crop, you go broke.

Scene 11: Astounding Courage

SX: car horn and travel.

Slide: car stuck in mud.

MPJ: I'm right on the main road and all the world goes past my door. Sometimes a dozen vehicles a day! Lots of horses. I see the homesteaders coming in.

Slide: two homesteader wagons.

All nationalities except British! It's rather thrilling to see them—the men and their wives and families—their stove, bedsteads, and pots and pans, and sometimes children's toys and violins and weird oddments on the wagon—an odd cow or two and an odd dog or two running behind. The whole procession moving at about three miles an hour.

Slide: child and dog in field.

There's something astounding about their courage. When they arrive, miles from anywhere, they've just got to camp out as best they can till the man has built them a house.

Slide: family in lean-to.

Did I tell you about the family I found in a tent—man, woman, and eleven children? The whole about two inches under water after the rain. The baby had whooping cough, and why in the name of wonder it hadn't also got pneumonia beat me. They'd only been there ten days, but the man had got his house as far as the roof. Pretty good work when his timber was four miles away.

Scene 12: Civilized Company

Slide: summer roadway.

MPJ: I went out to Mr. Maclean's

Slide: Mr. Maclean.

last night to get my hair cut. He's homesteading—but had worked in a barber shop once. He wasn't in,

Slide: Mrs. Maclean.

but his wife is a most attractive woman, and joy of joys,

Slide: piano keyboard.

she's got a piano!! It's the only piano, possibly within one hundred miles, and it's in good tune. I've a standing invitation to go and play. Hurrah! She is a city bred woman, and knows a lot of music I know.

SX: fade in "Moonlight Sonata."

So will you please send my music out—I want particularly: the Chopin "Nocturnes," the Rachmaninoff "Melodie,"

Slide: cross fade to "Moonlight Sonata."

the "Moonlight Sonata" . . .

Water break for MPJ, who may also put on frontier coat.

Scene 13: Arrival Of Brutus

SX: bark of big dog.

Slide: Brutus on hind legs.

MPJ: I've got my dog. He arrived just a week ago. Brutus.

He's simply enormous.

When I bought him, he was a little puppy, about half the size of our dog at home. Now he's as big as a collie and only four months old! You can imagine the amount of destruction a playful young elephant could do at 7 Ednam Road? Well, I assure you it's nothing to what Brutus did in half an hour here! He has to live outside.

Scene 14: Keeping Up

Slide: blank. MPJ starts to take off her jacket, and drops it off of playing space, seems unsure.

MPJ: I've got three patients to see tomorrow, fourteen miles riding. It's a great life, I assure you. But this business of housekeeping in my spare time is no joke.

Slide: portrait of Mother.

I've got Mother's photo over my kitchen table, and she always looks at me so reproachfully if I go out without doing the washing up! I did some washing ten days ago—the things are still rolled up waiting for ironing! And as for letter writing—the heap of unanswered letters grows higher with every mail.

Mary removes her skirt, to reveal trousers underneath.

I'm browner and stronger than I've ever been in my life. I'm almost the colour of an Italian now. Although I've been doing my own cooking, I'm not starving yet! It's a matter of fact I'm rather a good cook. You should just see my pastry! Mother herself couldn't beat it.

Scene 15: Cemetery

Slide: telegraph poles being installed.

MPJ: September 10.

The telegraph line is only twenty miles away now, and they will be up to here next week. I'll send you a cable perhaps for Christmas—right from here! Oh, we are getting civilized. We're even getting a cemetery!

Slide: cemetery.

They'll need one if I go on at this rate—three deaths in two months! It's become the stock joke—"Oh, we're getting on awful fast—first we got a doctor and now we've got a cemetery." I must say, I'm a little tired of it!

Scene 16: Shooting

Slide: blank.

SX: single shot.

MPJ: My shooting is abominable.

SX: three shots in quick succession, but a bit ragged.

It's worse than that. I only know of one worse shot in Canada—

Slide: men with guns and dog. She points to one of the men.

Dubé the garage keeper. It's rumoured that he took fifty shots to get four chickens the other evening! But I've been out for an hour this evening and achieved nothing. Not a feather. And I did want a chicken for supper. I missed about six, and I startled about twenty. Nearly trod on two. I have to leave the pup at home when I go shooting—he believes in fair play for the chickens, and goes ahead and warns them all!

Scene 17: First Snow

Slide: fresh snow on the ground.

MPJ: Snow—September 20. Well, that's about when they said we should have it.

I'm rather thrilled. It's the beginning of the really exciting part of this adventure. So far, I've only been playing with it. One gets so used to conditions up here that they become hardly noticed. It's only when people come along and gush over me that I feel that there is anything particularly out of the ordinary. It's usually parsons and such like from Toronto who come and spout about "pioneers" and "our great Empire" and take photos of me.

Scene 18: Mrs. Spivak

Slide: Mrs. Spivak and children.

MPJ: The Spivak baby has made the most dramatic recovery I have ever seen. Mrs. Spivak is a young nice-looking and well-educated Russian woman. She doesn't talk English much, but is picking it up quickly. She has the baby, three weeks old, and there are three other young children.

The shack is right in the middle of the bush, and you can't see another house from it. Mr. Spivak went off to Grimshaw about ten days ago—leaving his wife and ten-day-old baby quite well. The baby began to be ill, and for three days was getting worse.

Mrs. Spivak was alone with a sick baby, three small children, and absolutely no help till Mrs. Simpson, a mile away, happened to send her children round for some eggs. They went back and told her. Mrs. Simpson went over and found the

The Spivak family, 1929.
FAMILY COLLECTION

baby in convulsions. Mercifully, she's one of those intelligent people who know what to do for most emergencies. By that time I got there, the infant had been in an almost continuous convulsion for twelve hours, and was absolutely at its last gasp. That's what pioneering involves for women with children.

Scene 19: Not Winter Yet

Slide: winter vista or blank slide.

MPJ: It's not winter yet. The Chinook has been blowing steadily. But today the wind has gone round to northwest, and the thermometer is dropping fast, so we may be going to get snow.

Slide: northern lights 1.

The northern lights tonight are more wonderful than ever I've seen them. They spread across the whole sky, like a great bunch of streamers starting in the northeast and waving about in all directions. I can see them from every window.

Scene 20: Just A Slight Cold

Slide: two men at cabin or tent.

MPJ: I went out three days ago to see a man with pneumonia. While I was there, another homesteader came by—a Yankee who arrived two weeks ago. He was living in a tent and had caught a bad cold. Oh, a frightful cold, he said. He thought it might turn to pneumonia too, but was quite sure that he'd be cured with a drink of gin. But when he discovered that (A) I did not stock gin, and (B) though I was a government doctor, he had to pay for my services, he decided that it was only a slight cold, and was already getting better!

Scene 21: Big

Slide: lake and hills.

MPJ: There's something overwhelming about the size of Canada. I get the sensation sometimes that people are tiny beings, struggling with their backs to the wall against something that is bound to beat them. And when I see acres of land cleared and broken I feel a queer sort of triumph and then, seeing the Battle River country from one of the hills, I realize what a little scratch on the surface it is, and all round, shutting it in on every side, is bush and forest and muskeg, unmapped and untouched.

Not only that it is big, but that you can't help feeling all the time how big it is. Even though you can't see more than a mile or so around, you still feel that it goes on for thousands of miles. It seems to be something apart altogether from one's knowledge of geography. Do you get what I'm driving at, or does it sound merely mad?

SX: kettle whistle or bubbling.

Slide: log cabin interior.

Kettle's boiling. I'd better wash up.

Oh, you pampered beings who get hot water by turning the tap, you should just try this life! Getting water from a half frozen river is really exciting.

Slide: film clip of frozen stream.

You see, the ice gets thinner and thinner as you get nearer the water. It's hopeless unless there's a handy rock. Well, there are lots of rocks, but they're awfully awkwardly arranged! Also, standing on a rounded rock covered with a thin layer of ice while you reach over to get a bucketful of water is no mean balancing feat, I assure you. Even when you've got your water, turning round on aforesaid slippery rock and then stepping from one slippery rock to another to get to the bank has its excitements. I went through yesterday. I mean one foot only, but goodness, it was cold.

Scene 22: A Very Long Day

Slide: serene winter landscape.

MPJ: Thursday, November 21, 1929.

Yesterday morning, I lay in bed, gazing at a snow-covered world, thanking heaven that I hadn't anybody really ill on my list. I got up and made my breakfast, and before I'd eaten two spoonfuls of porridge, a car arrived. Patient was a boy of thirteen—Hungarian—whose "throat was swollen inside." Tonsillitis. Temperature one hundred and three. I looked at his chest, and sure enough, scarlet fever!

I shot him off home to bed, and told them to come back and fetch me in an hour's time. There wasn't room for three in the Ford.

Hurried to finish my breakfast, got as far as bacon and eggs and another car arrived. The little Frenchman from the garage, with frozen feet. Silly idiot was wearing leather shoes. Thawed those out. Fed him on cake and coffee, washed up, dispensed the necessary medicine, throat paint, serum, disinfectant for the scarlet fever kid, and just got done before they arrived for me.

Went and inspected the isolation and sanitary arrangements.

Warned them they were liable to a hundred dollar fine if they left their quarter section or allowed anyone else to enter it, put up a large quarantine notice, and gave the other kids serum all round. Then went and saw a kid with pneumonia who only lived one and a half miles from there.

Went home to find a message awaiting me that George Robertson's baby was very ill, and that Joe Hanson who lives next door to George Robertson had pneumonia. The temperature was below zero, and dropping rapidly.

I was hauling in some wood to keep the heat going while I was away, when another car arrived—the little Frenchman again. He'd left a pair of gloves in the morning. Hearing where I was off to, he offered to take me in his car, but warned me he'd broken his battery during the day and so he had no lights! I assured him that I knew that trail so well that I could find my way blindfolded.

But it's one thing to find your way along a well marked cart-track on horseback, and altogether another to pick out the way when it's entirely covered by snow and no one has been along it, and in a car going fairly quickly. However, we got there quite safely. It was only just six o'clock and not very dark. Sure enough, Mr. Hanson had pneumonia. Temperature one hundred and four point five. Looking after him took about an hour. He's a bachelor and had only been looked after by two other old bachelors who happened along. It took me about a quarter of an hour just to make his bed. It was just a jumble of blankets and coats.

It's a great life, having to do the nursing as well as the doctoring! You should have heard the other two old blighters enquiring if I'd come and tuck them up if they were ill! I threatened them with a dose of castor oil and they shut up.

Then I went and saw George Robertson's baby. It was pretty bad, and took me another half hour, so by the time we started back it was 7:30, absolutely dark, no stars—moon not up. We slid backward down two steepish hills, and had to back and take another run at them. In fact we had to do that three times at the second, and did an elegant sideways skid whose real beauty I didn't appreciate till I saw the tracks today!

I do see life, don't I?

Scene 23: Bedside Manner

Slide: blank.

MPJ: I've already seen a number of most interesting cases.

Slide: X-ray machine.

I begin to feel the difference in working away from a hospital with X-rays and a lab. I saw a case yesterday I'd have given anything to get X-rayed. I'm afraid it is hopeless anyway. The man will die whichever it is, but I'd have loved to settle the diagnosis.

Scene 24: Gossip

Slide: blank.

MPJ: Now I'm getting to know people, all the gossip is so much more interesting. The latest excitement is that Jim Schamehorn

Slide: "Jim Schamehorn" on left side of screen.

has shot four of Bill Grey's

Slide: "Bill Grey" on right side of screen.

pigs that were on his land. Well, that sounds straightforward—till you know that Jim's

Slide: "Jim Schamehorn" and "Lucy" on left side of screen.

daughter, Lucy, ran off last Christmas Eve to marry Bill's

Slide: "Bill Grey" and "Ned" on right side of screen.

son Ned. She

Slide: "Lucy."

ran away because they absolutely refused to allow her

Slide: "Ned."

to marry him. He is a half-breed and a Catholic.

Slide: "Jim" and "Mrs. Schamehorn."

They are Canadians of German extraction and virulent Protestants, and have a violent aversion to "breeds." Now, her father and mother won't have anything to do

Slide: "Lucy" and "Ned," right side of screen.

with her, and she won't have anything to do with them, though they live on adjacent sections.

My own situation is rather delicate. When Lucy increased the population with a boy,

Slide: whole picture of MPJ with "Lucy" and baby, right side of screen.

she still wouldn't have her mother in the house. Mrs. S.

Slide: "Mrs. Schamehorn."

used to waylay me on the road to enquire about

Slide: MPJ and "Lucy."

the infant, and Lucy didn't want me to give

Slide: add "Mrs. Schamehorn."

her mother any information. And when I told Mrs. S. what a lovely baby it was, she snorted and informed me it was a "breed."

Slide: add in whole family and pigs, surrounding MPJ holding baby.

Feelings won't be improved by this pig-shooting business.

Scene 25: Dentistry

Slide: blank.

MPJ: I've spent most of the morning pulling teeth.

Slide: frontier dentistry kit.

A man walked twenty miles in the snowstorm yesterday. He wanted ten teeth removed. My hat!

Slide: same kit, closer up.

Nearly all the crowns had gone, leaving just black stumps, and there were great abscesses all over the place. The roots of the canines were nearly an inch long and the others very little shorter!

Slide: same kit, close up on the pliers.

And when I'd done it, he'd got to walk twenty miles back! However,

SX: clank of tooth dropping into pan or onto table.

I got 'em out all right. Thank God I'm not a dentist!

Scene 26: First Real Cold

Slide: heavy snowfall.

MPJ: Monday it was minus thirty-five degrees. Tuesday it dropped to minus forty-five and a north wind blowing. You can have no conception how cold that is.

You don't feel cold—you just freeze. And the agony of thawing out frozen fingers beats anything I've felt. You feel so utterly helpless, very tired and weak and tearful. It's a ridiculous sensation. I've had a really hard week, four nights up, a slow maternity case, any amount of travelling in sleighs.

Slide: bundled in sleigh.

I got awfully sleepy from missing so many nights, and keeping awake in the sleigh was an awful effort. And yet to have gone to sleep any time would have been almost certain to lead to pretty severe frostbite.

Slide: frontier oven.

My house keeps warm enough, but I have to stoke the fire two or three times during the night. Even with the fire on day and night, I still had to thaw out the ink to fill my pen before writing this.

Scene 27: Christmas Cake

SX: period Christmas carols.

Slide: Christmas cake or Christmas pudding.

MPJ: Tuesday, December 24.

The pudding and sweets came up by Thursday's mail. Pudding basin broken but pudding intact, praise be! I also received a magnificent Christmas cake from Auntie Edie. I wish she could have seen the expressions on sundry old bachelors' faces when they tasted it. Cake like that has never been seen before in Battle River Prairie! I regret to say it's nearly all gone. I've had an awful lot of visitors lately!

Slide: film of sleigh ride.

No need to fear about my having Christmas "all on my lonesome!" I'm going out every day next week, and I've mortally offended lots of people by accepting other people's invitations first.

Scene 28: Brutus Rising

SX: big dog bark.

Slide: Brutus, sized proportionate to actor.

MPJ: Brutus is one of the most attractive dogs I've ever met. I can't imagine life without him.

He sits beside me at meals, and says "Please" most politely when I offer him anything, and won't touch it till he's been told he can have it. He'll even hold a biscuit in his mouth without chewing till he's told he can. But I can't get him to do that with meat yet.

He's just the right size for a dog team now. He did forty miles in thick snow the other day, and was quite fresh and chirpy at the end.

More than I was—I got frostbitten.

Scene 29: Professional Development

Slide: Metis family photos.

MPJ: I've had awfully interesting cases lately. I have spent half this afternoon peering down a microscope hunting for TB, and finding it. The amount of TB up here is horrifying.

Slide: small plane on ground, woman getting in.

I had a letter from Dr. Rodger today. She does have a thrilling life. Another aeroplane trip to Edmonton! I must be slow. All my patients seem to be capable of removal to hospital by less exciting means.

Scene 30: Dressing For The Cold

Slide: blank.

MPJ: Going for walks is anything but the simple thing it is in England. Before I can go out, I must put on about six layers of wool! Actually, a wool vest, woolen combs (ankle and elbow length), thick wool knickers, breeches, a thick wool sweater, a thick woolen coat, a moose hide coat, a thick camel hair and wool scarf, a wool cap with ear flaps, camel hair and wool mitts, and big fur and moose hide mitts coming almost to my elbows on top. And if I were going out in a sleigh I should add my big blanket, lined leather coat, my travelling rug, an enormously heavy travelling robe, and a charcoal heater for my feet. And even then probably get frostbitten!

Heather D. Swain as Mary Percy Jackson, with projections of Peace River and Dr. Sutherland, 2007. Photo of Dr. Sutherland courtesy of Peace River Museum and Archives.
IAN JACKSON/EPIC PHOTOGRAPHY

Scene 31: Fractured Skull

Slide: postcard of Peace River.

MPJ: McNamara Hotel, Peace River, Alberta, February 25.

Here I am in the "big city" again. I brought in a man with a fractured skull down to hospital in a caboose.

He was working on the telegraph outfit when a tree he was felling dropped onto his head. I was afraid he was bleeding inside his skull, but I haven't a trephine,

Slide: trephine.

only an amputation saw.

Slide: trephine and amputation saw.

We got him down here alive and Doctor Sutherland

Slide: Dr. Sutherland.

did some amazing surgery. He seems to have stopped bleeding, and though his pulse is only thirty-eight, he may recover.

Slide: tent on sleigh.

SX: jingle of harness—looped and looped till MPJ says "It looked so quaint . . ."

But he was difficult to look after, exceedingly irritable in spells. Tried to get up and go for a walk! All this in a small tent on the top of a rocking sleigh. We had to have a stove inside the tent of course. I was terrified that I should drowse off, and he'd sit up, and a jolt of the sleigh would send him head first into the heater!

Slide: northern lights 2.

It looked so quaint at night, the little tent, lit up inside, crawling over mile after mile of snow, with the northern lights shimmering and swaying above us, pale apple green and gold, edged with mauve. It was a perfect night.

Scene 32: Back To Civilization

Slide: blank slide.

MPJ: I hope to go down to Edmonton on Monday.

Slide: film clip of women crossing Jasper Avenue; end with still looking down Jasper Avenue.

I shall feel so funny in a city and wearing skirts. I'm really getting quite excited about going out and having a bath! Do you realize that I haven't had a bath for six months? I only hope I shan't get run over or anything. Really a city is awfully dangerous compared with the backwoods!

I'm going to have a busy time in Edmonton. I want to see what I can get out of the government, from a car to a hospital!

Then I want to see some ice hockey. And I shall have to go to the talkies and the theatre and any concerts. And shop of course.

Scene 33: Almost Famous

MPJ: The Corona Hotel, Edmonton.

I went to an ice-hockey match on Friday.

SX: hockey game.

Slide: hockey game from the period.

Edmonton versus Calgary. It was thrilling. If ever you get a chance to see one, don't miss it. The speed is amazing, and the whole thing terrifically exciting.

Slide: film clip of storm in Edmonton.

It's really very funny how things have changed since I arrived. I was just Dr. Percy then. Now I'm "Dr. Percy of Battle River" and everyone seems to know about me!

Slide: Edmonton Journal *headline.*

Would you believe it, the daily paper announced that I was arriving to attend the opening of Parliament! I'm getting an awful swelled head.

Scene 34: Dog Sledding

Slide: MPJ in dog sled.

MPJ: I have done quite a lot of travelling by dog team this week. It's an amazingly smooth comfortable way of travelling, and the speed is remarkable. It's very quiet. One lies at full length in the little sleigh and the sensation is almost like drifting downstream in a canoe, with the shosh of the sleigh on soft snow sounding like water.

Dogs are marvellous. I just lay down and drowsed and gazed at the stars and they found their own way. They'll follow a trail when it's under two feet of fresh snow.

Scene 35: Philistines

Slide: attractive shot of trees.

MPJ: They're going to cut down the spruce trees round the slough south of my house to build my barn. Isn't it tragic? It will spoil my beautiful view. But its no use arguing. They regard the slough as a blot on the landscape because it can't be cultivated! Even at night, when the trees cast queer black shadows on the snow by moonlight, they can't see it as anything but "that goddamn slough." Oh Lord—they're hopeless.

Scene 36: Beethoven

Slide: dark slide.

MPJ: Friday, March 28.

Oh, the winter is trying. For two pins I'd have dropped this job myself once or twice lately, but now spring is coming, I feel better.

You can't imagine the effect of the silence here at night. I've lain awake at New Milton listening to the quiet, and always there were lots of tiny sounds, but here it can be absolutely silent. Sometimes I stood outside, when I went to get in wood at night, and listened and listened and heard nothing except my own breathing. It was almost like some exceedingly refined Chinese torture!

Then I've gone in and put on the gramophone.

SX: Beethoven's "Fifth Symphony," loud movement.

Beethoven's "Fifth Symphony" usually, as a sort of protection against silence!

SX: cut music abruptly.

Don't think I'm going daft. I'm only trying to give you the sort of impression it makes.

Slide: green northern lights or green wash fading in.

SX: cut gramophone off.

I begin to hate the northern lights—they make the snow look such a queer greenish colour, and they swirl and wave so silently. I haven't felt like this very often, but it's a rather over-whelming sensation when it comes, one feels so insignificant and helpless, as if the whole of nature is antagonistic.

Scene 37: The New Teacher

Slide: school house interior.

MPJ: The school had a man teacher last year. The new school year starts in April. The trustees were so keen on having a woman that they didn't even bother about her qualifications! There are several bachelors among the trustees and of course they got a good deal of ragging. The real reason they wanted a woman was so that they could have things all their own way. The man was not very easy to manage.

When a wire came that she was coming, the excitement was really terrific.

Slide: spruced up older men.

Can't you just see them? All the old bachelors in the district shaved and spruced up and waiting at the store to greet the lady. And then their faces when the teacher arrived—

Slide: young man in suit.

and it was a *man*!

Scene 38: Hardy Ukrainians

Slide: MPJ on horseback.

MPJ: I've just come back from another maternity case. I got called out at 6:00 AM, collected my tools, and arrived at the place at 6:50 AM, to find the baby born, washed, and the lady energetically scrubbing the floor! She was planning to get breakfast next and then do the washing. I told her, in signs as she speaks no English, to go to bed, but she didn't want to. When I told her husband she should to go to bed for seven days, he translated and they both roared with laughter!

They are Ukrainians of the poorer type, living in a mud hut. The furniture consists of a stove, a plank bed covered with straw, and a shelf with a cup, a saucepan, and a pie dish. No table and no chairs. I expect they have some food somewhere, but I didn't see any.

Slide: young Ukrainian immigrants.

It seems to me that even though the numbers of emigrants from central Europe are limited to keep a higher proportion of English and Scandinavian peoples, yet before long the Slavs will be the dominant race in this part of Canada.

Slide: film of Ukrainian woman and chickens; recut to freeze on two women at the end.

They're tough and they're prolific, and they can make a success of farming on land no English man would touch.

They never believe in paying when they haven't got to. I do something, tell them how much, and they say "No have got Mrs. Doctor, thank you, goodbye." You should see their expressions when I get them to split wood! Or demand payment in eggs or butter!

Slide: small container of eggs.

This payment in eggs is getting rather a nuisance. When eggs were fifty cents a dozen it was all right,

Slide: more eggs.

but now they're down to twenty to twenty-five cents, and the price for pulling one tooth is four dozen eggs, it's getting serious!

I pulled three teeth for a Ukrainian woman the other day, and she's going to give me eggs!!!

Slide: a lot more eggs.

Scene 39: Dysentery

Slide: poling in swampy water.

MPJ: I'm fed up. I've got an outbreak of dysentery from drinking creek water. The creek is fouled by barns, stables, pig sties, privies, and manure heaps, and it's the only source of drinking water in that region.

I did a sanitary inspection with a policeman yesterday, and am making people shift their pig sties and barns. Gosh! Shan't I be popular? Some are oldtimers whose barns have stood there for five or ten years. But it didn't matter when no one lived below them. There were less than three hundred people in here three years ago. Now there are fifteen hundred, and more coming in every day.

Scene 40: Brutus In Disgrace

Slide: Brutus sitting up, to scale with MPJ, centre bottom of screen.

SX: dog whine or bark.

MPJ: Brutus has disgraced himself today. For the first time in his life, he took food off the table. To be sure it was afternoon and he hadn't been fed all day and I had started to eat a cake.

I left it on the table, and had forgotten all about it. Still, that doesn't excuse him. He's chained up outside now, very apologetic and sorry for himself when I go out.

He is still growing, in intelligence as well as size, and is a marvellous watchdog. He's ridiculously affectionate, rubs himself against me like a cat (almost knocking me over in the process) and will sit for hours with his head resting on my knees when I'm reading.

Scene 41: Egg Formula

Slide: young Ukrainian immigrants.

MPJ: You remember me telling you about a Ukrainian woman whose baby was born with extraordinarily little fuss before I arrived? A couple of weeks ago, she and her husband got dysentery. They've recovered, but when I called in, I found her spoon feeding the baby with a horrible-looking yellow fluid. Couldn't imagine what it was. She speaks no English practically, but she managed to explain that the dysentery had stopped her breast milk. They had no money to buy canned milk. None of their neighbours had a cow, so she was feeding the child on raw egg. The child looked perfectly well and happy on it too. But when you come to think of it, what else could she have done?

Scene 42: Politics Made Easy

Slide: political poster from 1930.

MPJ: It's election day! I'm not sure whether I shall vote. I know all the candidates but very little about the politics. It's all so mixed up with religion. All the Catholics vote Liberal. According to the Protestants, and particularly those from Saskatchewan, the Catholics are trying to make Canada a Catholic country, importing Catholic emigrants and then insisting on their voting Liberal so that they get into power.

It is a certain fact that if you want a Dominion job you'd better be a Catholic and if you want a provincial job you've got to be a Protestant.

Scene 43: Gardens

MPJ: There are no apple, pear, or cherry trees out here.

Slide: berries.

But the wild strawberry, raspberry, Saskatoon berry, gooseberry, black currant, and choke cherry all look very hopeful. There is a tremendous amount of wild strawberry about.

Slide: berry scoop.

People pick hundreds of pounds of them for bottling and jam. Unless the poorer people bottle wild fruit they will have none to eat for nearly eight months of the year. So they get hundreds of quart glass sealers and bottle a moose early in the spring, which gives them their meat supply for the summer. As they empty the jars they fill them with wild fruit, pickles, and vegetables. If the man is anything like a shot they have occasional prairie chicken, duck, goose, grouse, deer, and moose, so living is possible on extraordinarily little money, considering the high cost of groceries.

It's taken me a year to learn all these things; if I'm not too busy to bottle fruit myself this summer I shall be able to live very much more luxuriously next year.

Scene 44: Brutus III

Slide: Brutus with MPJ.

MPJ: Brutus has distemper very badly. I'm afraid he's dying. He's been in bed since Monday and is getting steadily worse. He's had nothing to eat and drink at all for forty-eight hours. I can't even pour water into him. It's heartbreaking.

I've had a terrible week, frightfully busy, very hot, eighty to ninety in the shade, and the mosquitoes worse than you can imagine. I'm absolutely played out today. It's 4:30 PM now but still too hot to ride, and I've thirty-six miles to cover in visits today. I didn't get back till 4:00 AM so couldn't get up early. I've had to leave Brutus at home all week and so have not been here to coax him to eat when he wasn't quite so weak.

Slide: fade to black.

If he dies I don't know what I shall do.

I can't imagine life here without him.

Scene 45: Residential School Epiphany

MPJ: Dear, dear! I never told you about the Indian reserve at Kinuso, or the Indian boarding school on Slave Lake, did I?

Slide: residential school exterior.

The Indian school is an amazing place. Catholic of course, and state supported. It looks like a huge hotel, with lots of windows, painted white and green. The old priest is French, unshaven, amazingly fat, and incredibly dirty, but a delightful old chap for all that. He breeds silver foxes in his spare time! He's quite the most worldly priest I've ever met.

The nuns who run the place and do all the teaching are equally surprising; young, bright, very thrilled with the new radio someone had just presented, chatted brightly to the men, in fact were normal teachers but most abnormal nuns. They took us all over the place.

Slide: school classroom.

There are one hundred and twenty little Indian kids there, all ages from four to sixteen. Poor little beggars! It's a lovely school, but you can't wonder that they hate it.

Slide: teepee.

Who wouldn't sooner sleep rolled in a blanket beside a fire in a great forest, than in a little white bed in a dormitory? And such a dormitory.

Slide: night view of residential school.

Doubtless the cubic space per child is correct, but the floor space isn't. There is just room to walk between beds, and there are fifty or sixty beds in a room. The ceiling is very high, but the rooms look so overcrowded. The children are only allowed to speak English. Poor little kids! You know it seems rather terrible to see the "noble red-man" being cooped up.

Slide: immigration poster 1.

You know I can't help feeling that we gloss over the bad behaviour of the British in history, and only draw attention to the good we did in some parts of the world. Hang it all! What right had we to wipe out the inhabitants of North America? They never did us harm. They were happy enough living their own lives and were a fine and healthy race. Then we come along and seize parts of their country and live in it and because they fight, send out armies and slaughter them, driving them back to the west. Then trade with them and give them alcohol and religion, and subsequently proceed to shut them up on little reserves, while we divide up their country amongst the surplus population of Europe.

Slide: progress of railroad.

Now, although we've thousands of square miles of unoccupied land, we gaze with covetous eyes on the Indian reserves because they are good land. Kinuso is very anxious to get rid of its reserve. It's a patch of good land stretching from the railroad to the lake. Two reserves north of the Peace River were sold this summer. I suppose the same thing happened in Australia and New Zealand and to a smaller extent in South Africa.

Yet when I read it as history I rejoiced over the victories against the horrible scalping tomahawking Red Indian.

Just a few days after arriving in Alberta, Dr. Jackson was sent out with a travelling
medical centre. She was delighted with her first real contact with local wildlife.

Scene 46: Brutus Improves

SX: deep barks.

Slide: Brutus up and begging.

MPJ: I'm glad to say Brutus is very much better.

He began to improve last Monday and for the last few days I could hardly keep up with his appetite. He's desperately thin. I've had to take up his collar six inches!

Scene 47: Off To The Mountains

Slide: postcard image of mountains.

MPJ: July 27.

I am immensely thrilled about my upcoming alpine holiday. I was beginning to get bad-tempered and snappy, and I had three septic fingers, one after another. Not bad, but enough to be annoying.

Scene 48: Climbing

Slide: rail line into mountains.

MPJ: Canadian Alpine Club, Maligne Lake Camp, Jasper, Wednesday, July 30.

Slide: Maligne Lake.

This is the most marvellous place imaginable for camping out. It's at the south end of Maligne Lake, fifty miles from Jasper, on a little flat dotted with spruce trees. The lake a deep greeny-blue in front, and high snow-capped mountains behind. The lake is fed by glacier streams and one can hear the roar of the falls. Yesterday, I got up at 6:00 AM to go for "a scramble up the Thumb." It's the nearest mountain, towers right over the camp. When we lined up to start I discovered

Heather D. Swain as Mary Percy Jackson, 2007.
IAN JACKSON/EPIC PHOTOGRAPHY

that there were six of us. The other five were all climbers, and two Swiss guides! It was obvious that they wouldn't be sending guides with the sort of scramble I'd been expecting, but I didn't like to back out.

Slide: less vertical climbing shot.

It's only nine thousand and two hundred feet high. It's the lowest peak in this region, and is considered only a scramble by these folks. But they consider "The Matterhorn" only a tourist climb. For me it felt like real mountaineering.

Slide: more vertical climbing shot.

We zigzagged across steep patches of sliding scree—negotiated a snow cornice—were roped up and climbed up a patch of almost smooth rock and then were pushed and pulled round a corner of rock with singularly awkward foot—holds and a thousand foot drop if you fell. Then did about a quarter mile up steep snow, a good bit steeper than a house roof, up steps made by the guide. Along a fairly wide snow edge—eighteen inches—with a drop to eternity on either side, and finally achieved the top.

Slide: men at top of mountain.

We came down a different way—much more snow. We all sat and tobogganed down a thousand feet of it! A perfectly marvellous sensation, till you come to thin snow and feel the rocks!

Slide: blank.

I tore six holes in the seat of my breeches, and they got filled with snow, but it was great fun. It's taken two and a half hours to mend them this morning!

Scene 49: Back From Vacation

Slide: front of locomotive.

MPJ: Soon my holiday will be over. I'm writing this in a very shaky train, and hope you'll be able to read it.

Slide: elegant rail car interior.

It's a really elegant train. I'm in a drawing room panelled in silver sycamore and ebony with imitation Lalique glass lamp shades, silver chair covers, and a radio.

Then there is a barber and a bath and basins of green porcelain and a vibro-massage apparatus! Talk about the ancient Romans!

Slide: home on hilltop.

Ah, but it's marvellous to be going back to a house by the river, sleeping out in a hammock slung between birch trees on the bank.

Slide: view from house.

To a dog and a horse and swimming and riding and shooting and fishing. Do you wonder I can't face coming back to England yet?

Slide: film clip of man on steps of legislature, followed by blank slide.

Have seen Dr. Bow and the minister of health. There has not been time to discuss salaries, they say. They will write me. But I think I shall come back, even if I don't get a dollar rise! Honestly, I hate the thought of quitting. You see, there is no one to take my place. Canadian doctors of either sex just will not go. The only reasons Canadian men doctors are found in the wilds are drink, dope, or incompetence,

Slide: Dr. Sutherland.

with—of course—a few brilliant exceptions like Dr. Sutherland in Peace River. Hence the English women they sent for.

Slide: MPJ with one family.

> Of course, the salary is not large, but in a year I've gained a reputation that I might never have got in a lifetime in England. And above all, the work is worth doing.

Slide: accumulated images of patients from the slides.

SX: "Moonlight Sonata."

> I'm still not much further ahead with answering letters, so I won't spend any more time on this. There's no news anyway.

Slide: MPJ signature.

Slide: black.

End

Interior of the Ernest Brown Photography Studio, on Jasper Avenue.

THE UNMARRIED WIFE

THE PASSION AND PHOTOGRAPHY OF GLADYS REEVES AND ERNEST BROWN

BY KAREN SIMONSON AND DAVID CHEOROS

Heather D. Swain as Gladys Reeves and Mark Anderako as Ernest Brown,
in front of the recreation of the Ernest Brown Photography Studio at
Fort Edmonton Park. Promotional photo for the original production, 2009.
NICOLE DIEBERT

GLADYS REEVES

Gladys Reeves was born in June 1890 in Somerset, England. The youngest daughter of William Paris and Clara Ellen Gold Reeves, the family moved to Edmonton in 1904. Gladys began working for Ernest Brown Limited in 1905. In 1920, she established her own photographic studio, The Art League. The studio and her apartment were destroyed by fire in February 1929. Also destroyed were many of Ernest Brown's historical negatives that Gladys was storing. She re-established her studio over the Empress Theatre in Edmonton and it remained open until 1950.

Gladys was a member of the Edmonton Horticultural Society and was also instrumental in the Edmonton Tree Planting Committee, which was responsible for planting over five thousand trees in boulevards throughout Edmonton in 1923. Gladys Reeves died April 26, 1974, at the age of eighty-three and was cremated, with her ashes interred at Westlawn cemetery.

ERNEST BROWN

Ernest Brown was born September 8, 1877, in Middlesborough, Yorkshire, England. He studied photography in Newcastle-on-Tyne. He married Mary Molly Carr in 1902. Their daughter, Winnifred Dolly, was born and died in 1905, and their son, Alan, was born in 1909. Ernest set out for Canada in 1903, spending some time in Toronto, but unable to find work. He learned of a job as assistant to Edmonton's first photographer, C.W. Mathers, and moved to the city in 1904.

Not long after beginning his job with Mathers, Brown bought the rights to Mathers's portrait studio, and the rest of the business in 1907. In 1905, he expanded the studio into Ernest Brown Limited.

In 1912, his new building, the Ernest Brown Block, was opened. After the First World War, Brown fell on hard times and his business was seized in 1920. He ran as a candidate for the Independent Labour Party in 1921 and published a short-run reformist newspaper called the *Glow Worm*.

In 1926, Brown moved to Vegreville and took over the Vegreville photographic studio, which was primarily run by an assistant. His focus had changed to trying to promote and sell images from his collections. He returned to Edmonton in 1929. From 1933 until 1939, Brown operated the Pioneer Days Museum in Edmonton. In 1947, he sold his photographic collections to the Alberta government for fifty thousand dollars. Brown died January 3, 1951, and is buried in the cemetery on Seventh Avenue.

The Unmarried Wife premiered at the Roxy Theatre, Edmonton, Alberta, on July 28, 2009, with the following company:

Alan Brown (Alan)	Mark Anderako
Ernest Brown (EB)	Mark Anderako
Gladys Reeves (GR)	Heather D. Swain
Molly Brown (Molly)	Heather D. Swain

Director	David Cheoros
Costume Designer	Geri Dittrich
Lighting Designer	Paul Bezaire

The production ran approximately fifty minutes.

Heather D. Swain as Gladys Reeves and Mark Anderako as Ernest Brown, with Ernest Brown's original desk at Fort Edmonton Park. Promotional photo for the original production, 2009.

NICOLE DIEBERT

SET

A bare stage is used. Locations are evoked using projections of images from the Ernest Brown and Gladys Reeves Photograph Collections in the Provincial Archives of Alberta.

COSTUMES

Gladys Reeves wears a simple dress, adding a sweater for the final scene. Ernest Brown/Alan Brown wears a dark suit. Both are appropriate for 1961, but resonate with an earlier period.

Scene 1: The Funeral

January 16, 1961, at the reception following Molly Brown's funeral. Alan Brown is fifty-two. Gladys Reeves is sixty-nine.

GR: I'm so sorry.

Alan: Oh, hello Miss Reeves.

GR: Please, Alan. After so many years.

Alan: Gladys.

GR: The flowers were exquisite.

Alan: Um. Walter Ramsay's. They just sent over . . .

GR: Well, they did it right. The lilies bowing over the casket . . . and the service was very dignified. Well, until Thom MacDonald started singing "Amazing Grace."

Alan: If only he'd picked one key. *A shared laugh.* I didn't remember that women . . . bring food. I have so much beef stew. I was thinking of opening a restaurant.

GR: Molly would be so pleased with the service.

Alan: It was good of you to come.

GR: It was never a question. How are you doing?

Alan: Everyone always asks that. It's such a stupid question.

GR: I didn't—

Alan: My mother has just died—how am I supposed to feel? Gutted? Liberated? Fine? A fifty-two-year-old orphan. Makes me feel lonely.

GR: *Awkward silence.* How's your wife?

Alan: Norma is fine. A bit relieved, I think. Her life has revolved around looking after Mother the last few months.

GR : *Another awkward pause.* Are you still with Ferguson and Hrudley?

Alan: Yes. Still doing accounting there. It's been twelve years now. Hard to believe. *Another awkward pause.* Are you still gardening these days?

GR: Not as much as I used to. Not like back in the heyday of the Tree Planting Committee.

Alan: *After yet another awkward pause.* I am surprised you came.

GR: Why?

Alan: Well, you and Father—

GR: You Browns, all of you—we go back a long way. It was fifty-five years ago I first met your father . . .

Scene 2: First Job

Gladys, aged fifteen, enters Brown's storefront studio. Ernest is searching through a pile of glass slides. Gladys waits, looking at the "stuff" in the studio office.

EB: Where's that Turner negative?

GR: Excuse me.

EB: Confound it, man! Why can't I ever find anything around here!

Searches the room with his eyes. He hasn't really seen Gladys.

GR: Well, it does not help that you have got boxes of frames piled all over the place, your aisles are choked with frames on the floor, your desk is a bird's nest of papers.

EB: Can I help you, miss?

GR: I have been sent by my mother. To inform Mr. Brown that my sister, Alice Reeves, is not able to take the job with him, as she has found employment elsewhere. He should not expect a telephone call from her. Good day.

She turns away primly.

EB: Wait a minute. What do you do?

GR: *Surprised.* Me? I, ah, go to school.

EB: Well, aren't you big for school?

GR: My size has nothing to do with that. I am fifteen and am thinking I'd like to be a teacher. I received excellent marks in all my classes last year, and my teacher thinks I have a great talent. My favourite subject is history, but I also like mathematics.

EB: What are you doing now?

GR: I am on my holidays, which I am sick and tired of. There's nowhere to go.

EB: Would you like to come up and answer the phone and the door and let me get my work done? The pay is fifteen dollars a week.

She giggles her response. He smiles back.

Transition to 1961.

GR: My first job. Greet the customers, wrap up the framed pictures, answer the telephone, and type up correspondence. All because my sister decided to work as a receptionist somewhere else, my life changed.

Alan: Not just yours, I suppose.

GR: That was a very hard time for your parents. Dolly was already sick. I'd only been working for about a month when she died.

Alan: Born in January. Gone by September.

GR: I didn't even get to see her.

Alan: They never really told me about my sister.

Exterior view, the Ernest Brown Photography Studio.

GR: She'd been struggling for months. Not able to hold anything down. And your father was so busy at that time. He could barely concentrate. Yet that September was the birth of the province. Your father wasn't about to let that occasion go unphotographed.

Alan: Of course. Always business first.

Scene 3: Daughter Figure

Time shift to 1905. Gladys is fifteen.

GR: Is there any way I can help, sir?

EB: *Rushing around.* No, no, just mind the shop. So much to do . . . Capture the parade—and the inauguration ceremony. I need to make sure I get Governor General Grey. Prime Minister Laurier. Lieutenant-Governor Bulyea. Mayor MacKenzie. So many moments to capture.

GR: That's wonderful, but—

EB: People will want these images—such a historic event—it will change this part of the world forever, and I'll have it.

GR: You haven't had anything to eat—

EB: No, no. No time to stop.

GR: I could go see how Dolly is doing.

EB *Taken slightly aback.* Dolly? No, Molly would telephone if anything changed.

GR: Well, you know where I am if you need anything.

EB: Thank you.

Back to 1961.

GR: Dolly died a week after the inauguration. Ernest could barely function after her death. Your mother spent two weeks curled up on the floor of the baby's room. I managed to drag her away to Father's farm for a weekend. Seeing her feeding the chicks, riding for the first time.

Alan: Mother rode?

GR: Giggling like a child. I think that was the foundation of our friendship. Your mother and I did have a great friendship, in our way. There was a hollowed out place that Dolly left in her, even after you were born four years later. I'm not sure how they would have coped if I hadn't been there.

Alan: I remember a lot of photographs of you with them.

GR: You were too young to remember, but I was indispensable to Ernest Brown Limited. The business was growing. So many people wanted photographs taken.

Alan: I don't remember him around that much when I was young.

GR: He usually got home after you were in bed. He was trying so hard to make his business successful. We spent many late nights at the shop. I'd take care of the paperwork while your father developed negatives and printed photographs.

Alan: Mother used to say how Father relied on you. With the business.

GR: Well, I was good at it. That made it possible for all of you to travel back to England.

Alan: I wish I could remember something from that trip.

GR: You were, what—three? Your mother wrote to me nearly every day. I was the envy of the other girls, getting such a series of letters from overseas.

Scene 4: Christmas 1911

Letter from Molly.

GR: December 31, 1911, Darlington.

Hello Gladys. Another line or two. I seem as though I cannot get settled down to write the whole story. The parcel you mentioned in your last letter has not arrived. It will have to make haste to catch Mr. B as he leaves for good Tuesday. I don't like to think of it, although I suppose I'll get accustomed.

On Saturday, Mother, Mr. B, myself, and Alan went to Darlington. I saw two very nice dresses, one was black and the other a grey, heavy-looking material—I thought that they were quite a good price. We spent Christmas day at Sunderland, and the day after I took Alan through to Shields to my sister's. We are bound for London on Monday. We have promised to take Alan to the zoo. Mr. B's time is flying and I'm wondering what Alan will say when he is gone.

Now Gladys, I hope you are quite well. Well, bye-bye and be good until I come back. Night, night, love to you. Yours as ever, Molly Brown.

Alan: If you don't mind me saying, Miss . . . Gladys. It seems a strange kind of friendship that includes an affair with her husband.

GR: Molly was always so kind. I felt guilty at first. I'm not excusing what I—

Alan: What he—

GR: Your father was a man with tremendous passion, strong ideals and opinions. Even if I didn't always agree. I felt like he took up all the space in my life, and it was terrifying and wonderful. That's why I kept sending so many letters, and eagerly awaited the ones from him.

EB: January 9, 1912.

I sail from Avonmouth tomorrow. It is a long trip, and fraught with danger; it is at this time we look to the Supreme

Being to watch over us and take care of us. I am not going to write you a sermon, sweetheart. I know you don't like it.

I trust God will carry me safely over to you. That God will keep you, my wife, and my child from all harm and permit us all to meet again and to live more useful lives in the future. Some would say this may be blasphemy, if they knew our relationship. But God knows our hearts, and what man or woman dare lift a finger and say we are wrong.

The ministers in the marriage service say, "Those whom God have joined together let no man put asunder." God said, "I am the God of Abraham, the God of Isaac, the God of Jacob." Abraham, Isaac, and Jacob were commanded to take more wives. That law was not repealed. But the common law of the land says a man shall have but one wife. Who is right, the Bible or the common law?

And what is the result? I don't think God intended man to waste their substance, or yet to take a girl and neglect her. But to take her, to honour her and provide for her, is quite a different thing. I believe the biggest sin, one committed by most of married people, is the prevention of bringing children into the world. Race suicide. I would write you chapters on this subject but we have debated it too often before, and will again I hope. And I said I was not going to write you a sermon.

Molly certainly has sung your praises out here. I thank you, sweetheart, for the muffler you sent me. I wear it over my chest, which includes my heart, all the time—except when I am sleeping. Don't forget you are still my darling sweetheart yesterday—today—and forever; only God can change it. You are my unmarried wife now and for all eternity.

GR: Yours affectionately, Ernest Brown.

Alan: So, I wasn't even three, and he was already cheating on my mother. I had no idea it had started so early!

GR: You need to understand.

Alan: Understand?

GR: In 1912, everything seemed to be going his way. Business
        . . . family . . . Then he moved forward on his grand plan
        for a new building on Jasper Avenue—the Ernest Brown
        Block. So beautiful.

Alan: Now, every time I walk past it, it's a reminder of how far
        he fell.

GR: He had a flock of assistants working for him, and figured he
        was worth a quarter of a million dollars. Can you imagine—a
        quarter of a million dollars in 1914!

Alan: Does that excuse him?

GR: Of course not. But . . . your father developed different views
        to most people.

Scene 5: Losing The Business

Transition to EB dictating to GR, or possibly being coached by her.

EB: September 6, 1924.

GR: To whom it may concern:

EB: This photograph of the first legislature of Alberta has this day
        been purchased from me, Ernest Brown, to hang in the court
        house, in the city of Edmonton.

GR: It is therefore likely to be preserved from fire or destruction
        for some considerable time.

EB: A few observations may prove of interest in the years to come.
        I started in business—

GR: —As successor to C.W. Mathers—

Ernest Brown.

EB: —in 1904 and have all the photographic records of anything that happened in the West for forty years back. The people of today have no sentiment—

GR: —when it comes to paying money to back that sentiment.

EB: Consequently, my collections of records bring me no return whatsoever. Financially, I am now broke.

GR: Mortgage foreclosures have been so numerous that the loan companies have now possession of nearly all of the business blocks of the city.

EB: All progress contains within itself the seeds of its own destruction. The greed and avarice of the moneyed people will bring about their own fall.

I trust that in the future you will be enjoying the fruits of paper money issued by the government direct to the people, in sufficient quantities to answer all the requirements of trade.

GR: That you will have made some very great steps toward a co-operative commonwealth—

EB: —little spoken of or even dreamed about at this time except by a very few people.

GR: That our machine production of commodities will be in such quantities as to fill the requirements of every person who works.

Both: But no more.

EB: That all mortgage loans will be issued by the government.

GR: That there will be no need for life insurance companies, owing to a government system of providing for those unable to or past the age for work.

EB: That the word "interest" will be unknown to you.

That you will have a religion founded on the brotherhood of man.

That patriotism will have passed away and international brotherhood taken its place.

That the teaching of Jesus Christ will be practised and "Christianity" not "church"ianity will rule.

GR: That education will be as free as the air we breathe, and will develop the mind to think for itself instead of teaching what others say is right.

EB: That two hours per day instead of eight and ten as at present will constitute a work day, giving the people ample leisure to develop the talents with which nature has endowed them.

That you will have doctors to keep you well, not as at present deriving their income through your sickness.

GR: That birth control will be taught.

Both: That women will have come into their rightful place in the social order of things.

GR: That the institution of marriage . . .

EB: That the institution of marriage will be such that when two unsuited souls are joined together in matrimony there will be some comparatively easy way in which they may be divorced without one of the parties having to commit so called adultery. Sincerely, Ernest Brown.

Transition back to Gladys and Alan.

Alan: Oh, I know he had some odd beliefs. Especially after the war.

GR: He was a man of strong ideals. I admired him for that.

Alan: So did my mother.

GR: And they did try at their marriage. For you.

Alan: I remember one day, I woke up when he got home and slammed the door. I snuck out of my room. There was a place at the top of the stairs where you could hear absolutely everything going on in the kitchen.

Scene 6: End Of Marriage

Door slams as EB returns home from work.

Molly: Ernest? You're back earlier than usual. Did you have a good day at work? *No answer. More forcefully, knowing something is wrong.* How was your day, Ernest?

EB: It's all coming apart, Molly. I've gotten notice from the city. They've thrown me out. Out of my own building. It's extraordinary.

Molly: I'm sure everything will work out, Ernest.

EB: I'm sure it won't. But I'm free. I've spent two years now worrying about this very day, this very event, and now it's arrived. I feel . . . light.

Molly: Ernest, you're frightening me.

EB: You should try it, Molly. The thing that you worry about more than anything happens, and you just . . . keep breathing. Walking around. Talking. And so, lovely Molly, there's nothing left to do but what you want.

Molly: Ernest. No.

EB: Yes, darling. I'm moving out. You know that I've—

Molly: You said that you could keep it separate. You—you stood there and promised me!

EB: *Drastic change.* I am sorry Molly. We both know . . .

Gladys Reeves.

Molly: It was only a matter of time. You've seemed so distant for a long time now. *Pause.* Please, for appearances' sake, don't go running to Gladys. Not right away.

EB: I never meant to hurt you.

Molly: Oh, don't worry about me. I have Alan and—I'll be fine.

Back to 1961.

Alan: I couldn't understand what was happening. And why was Mother talking about you?

GR: Oh, Alan.

Alan: Well, neither of them talked about it in front of me, not for years. It wasn't something that got discussed in the twenties.

GR: It was hard. But your father provided for the house. I was proud of your mother when she got herself the job . . .

Alan: As a seamstress for Trudeau's. By the time I was twenty, I was the one who supported us.

GR: As much as your father fancied himself a great business-man, he wasn't the best at managing money and supporting a family.

Alan: I paid for the house, supported mother—her wages weren't that much. And then he went off to run that bloody studio in Vegreville.

GR: I think I spent more on stamps those years he was in Vegreville than the whole rest of my life.

Scene 7: Vegreville

GR: Sunday, November 13, 1926.

Well, Sweetheart Mine, Friday I left ten dollars in the till for change and there was less than five dollars at the end of the day, as we had bought paper and a few odd things. Saturday about ten dollars came in from school pictures and one dollar from a sitter. If the other photographers are doing a like proportion, some of them must be getting anxious.

Daddy—you don't realize how delighted I am to think that you are at last coming into your own. The views are distinctly yours and no one has any right to them but you. I realize what a new and bright avenue it opens up for you. You can be much happier in your work and not just marking time.

I'm so sorry you weren't able to come to town this weekend, but will look for you on Friday evening, rain or shine.

I love you very much, and will always be your own, Gaga.

GR rushes over to hug and kiss him. It's late on a Friday night—EB coming to Edmonton for the weekend.

EB: Hello to you, too.

GR: I wish I could come meet you at the train station. It's agony waiting here for you.

EB: *Touching her cheek.* I know, Gaga. But we can't be too public. Alan's just finishing school. He gets enough teasing as it is. Thank goodness for this cozy little love nest on Jasper.

GR: I couldn't have stayed with my family any longer, especially with you away. Where would we have met?

EB: This is just perfect.

GR: I've got dinner all ready. All your favourites.

EB: Wonderful, I'm famished.

GR: And guess what? I've told everyone who's asked that business held you up in Vegreville, and you weren't going to be able to come into town this weekend. So there's no one to see. We can hole up here until Sunday afternoon.

EB: I'll just sneak in a quick visit in with Alan and Molly.

GR: What?

EB: I should really go see my wife and son.

GR: I heard you the first time. Why do you need to?

EB: That seems obvious.

GR: They don't know even know you're here. Can't you just stay here with me?

EB: They're my family.

GR: And what am I then?

EB: *Pause.* The love of my life.

GR: Doesn't feel like it.

EB: I won't be gone long. You can come if you like.

GR: No, I always feel the thermometer drop when I join you on those visits. Can't imagine why.

EB: Oh, Gaga. My dear, dear Gaga. I'm sorry. *Brings her in to hug; she struggles a bit, but eventually gives in. Let's* not spoil this weekend by arguing. I'll visit them for a little bit tomorrow afternoon. The rest of the weekend is ours. Did you have anything in particular in mind? *Twinkle in his eye. She chuckles and tickles him, breaking the embrace.*

Transition to 1961.

GR: Alan, you saw the stern British patriarch, but he was my great passion.

Slide: letter.

GR: Hello Daddy Pop-Old Honey-Bunch. I have a fierce head-ache, but haven't had any supper yet. I should probably go to sleep early. I wish I had my Lover to cuddle in to. Never mind. We enjoy our brief visits, don't we, love? But the real good times are yet to come, years when we can enjoy each other's companionship to the full.

I'm kind of glad we were both financially up against it for a while. You see if you still had a business worth a quarter of a million, you might think it was an easy sitting that I wanted; but now you know it's you I want. If fortune favours us now, it will be ours, not yours or mine.

Have just remembered I must develop yesterday's and today's films before I go to bed; so will run to mail this now. It is past eight o'clock. Wish I could kiss you goodnight, but shall kiss you in my imagination instead. God bless you Lover. Your very own Sweetheart Gaga.

Alan: Miss Reeves. Perhaps my mother's funeral is not the best time for these stories.

GR: I'm sorry. I got caught up in the memories—

Alan: I'd like to be civilized enough to—

GR: Those four years he was in Vegreville were very difficult.

Alan: Well, they weren't any easier when family dinners were shoe-horned in between rolls in the hay.

She strikes him. There is a moment.

Alan: I suppose I deserved that.

GR: I suppose I did too.

Alan: Jealousy. I suppose it doesn't let go very easily.

GR: Pardon?

Alan: Jealousy.

GR: Well, your mother had some good reason to be jealous.

Alan: That wasn't what I meant.

GR: I don't understand.

Alan: Surely you . . . I had a huge crush on you. When I was a boy.

GR: On me? You're joking.

Alan: You were strong, and independent, and . . . tall.

GR: I thought you just blushed easily.

Alan: When Father came back from Vegreville, I had hoped that we'd see you more often.

GR: Alan.

Alan: But if anything, you were both busier than ever.

GR: Well, with the fire—

Alan: It must have been devastating.

GR: Hard to believe my business was up and running again within a month after the fire. I'd lost my business, my home, much of Ernest's collection.

Alan: Thank goodness he hadn't moved all of his furniture and photography supplies back from Vegreville yet.

GR: Losing part of his collection—it seemed to push Ernest even harder toward his work sharing his pictures with the world.

Alan: But he'd been doing that for years.

GR: But it was all consuming when he returned to Edmonton. He continued to use the Art League name. But by 1929, I didn't need to hide behind that name any longer. When I'd started out, I didn't think that people—men—would trust a lady photographer. But after almost ten years—I felt I could let that go. And Ernest needed it more, for promoting his vision.

Photo exhibit from the Pioneer Days Museum.
PROVINCIAL ARCHIVES OF ALBERTA, PRI974.0173/105E

Alan: All those boxes and boxes of postcards.

GR: Which lead him to want to expand the educational possibilities.

Both: Which lead to the museum.

Scene 8: Pioneer Days

GR: Good afternoon, class. Mr. Brown and I are delighted you have joined us today, and you're going to have an exciting time learning about the history of the West. As you can see from the displays around you, we have excellent photographs to show how things have changed over the last half century. Now, I'll turn it over to Mr. Brown to say a few things.

EB: To understand the present, and the possibilities of the future, in both our social and economic life, we must understand the conditions that went before.

The story of those who preceded us by many years should be interesting to anyone who has red blood in his veins.

It has been said that western Canada has no historic background; which may be true if compared with the ancient western civilizations.

GR: But wouldn't it be interesting to know where our Eskimos and Indians came from? We have much to learn about the folklore of the Natives.

EB: Their medicine lodge, sun dance, crucifixion, tribal habits, language, and customs.

Who were the hardy men who established the Forts with the stirring names of "Confidence," "Resolution," "Reliance," "Good Hope," and . . .

GR: "Providence."

EB: "Providence."

For a tale of endurance, fortitude, discipline, and tact, we have the march west of that splendid body of men the North West Mounted Police.

GR: The Mounties!

EB: Their scrimmages with the whisky traders and the Indians; the establishing of law and order, permitting railroad construction and settlement of the country.

GR: When we go into the country of the prairie section and look for miles and miles as far as the eye can see, over what appears like a vast ocean as seen three days from land.

EB: Then return to our towns and cities and observe the business blocks, the sky-scraping buildings, the homes with beautiful trees and garden. We constrain today with the poet: "I hold it as a truth that he who makes two blades of grass to grow where only one grew before, is a public benefactor, and deserves more of mankind than all the politicians put together."

GR: *Applauds to cut him off.* Okay, children. Please feel free to look around at the different photographs we have on display.

EB: This is a very important section. It shows Alberta's inauguration—when we became a province.

Slide: Laurier at the reviewing stand.

Prime Minister Laurier spoke about the West as an enduring legacy of promise and hope for all of Canada.

Slide: group shot on reviewing stand.

The Governor General's address was especially stirring. Yes, that was a time of great . . . celebration. *Ernest is lost in reverie.*

Slide: museum's advertising logo.

GR: Class, we hope you've enjoyed your visit to the museum. Remember to tell your parents . . . and tell them to come back with you.

Time shift to 1961.

Alan: That crazy museum of his.

GR: "Crazy museum of ours." And it wasn't so very crazy. It took up almost all his time, but people really liked it. All the nights spent rearranging things, tinkering with the exhibits. Hard work, but there were a few moments that made it all worthwhile.

Scene 9: Breakfast

GR: Would you like sausage with your eggs this morning, Ernest?

EB: Hmm, no, only toast for me.

GR: Okay, Daddy-pop.

GR brings over breakfast, maybe touching EB on the back as she gives him his breakfast and quick kiss on the cheek. Both begin to look at different section of the newspaper. GR, surprised.

> Oh. Here we are in the *Journal*. *Pause.* I'm a little afraid to go on.

EB: Oh, don't be silly, girl.

GR: Okay then. The editorial's titled, "Learning History from Pictures."

> "School children of Edmonton are discovering a deep interest in history through the photographs and other pictures collected by Mr. Ernest Brown." Apparently, I have nothing to do with it. "The other day, a Grade 8 class from one of the public schools visited the 'Pioneer Days' exhibit. Their teacher was amazed at the interest shown by the children. They were free to go home at four o'clock but most of them stayed until the exhibit closed at five."

EB: Does he give the address?

GR: "To be sure the exhibit is a 'commercial' venture—"

EB: Commercial!

GR: "—if the small fee charged visitors can be said to put it in that class. But the interest it is arousing in the boys and girls of Edmonton stamps it as a fine educational influence. Those who see the pictures find the history of the city and province beginning to live for them."

EB: "Beginning to live for them." I rather like that.

GR: "As one visitor, a well-known Alberta educationalist, remarked, the collection of pictures is well worth preservation by the government or some other agency."

EB: To suggest I part with my collection!

GR: Well, one day you might like to sell. Give you the money to travel.

EB: I've still got—

GR: You won't live forever.

EB: But I've got you to take care of it.

GR: I won't live forever either.

EB: Well, maybe if someone offered the right price. So much of my time has been put into arranging, rearranging, culling— to make it just right. That's not even mentioning how much it's taken to preserve these photographs for so many years. They're like my children.

Transition back to 1961.

Alan: Well, I'm glad something was like his children.

GR: Is that what you think? He was so proud of you. He couldn't stop talking about the job you landed at Ferguson and Hrudley.

Alan: Seriously?

GR: But, yes, he was fond of that museum. It had a good run. There was some movement to keep it going. The newspaper called the collection "priceless." One hundred thousand visitors in six years. Remember, the population was only ninety thousand at that time.

Alan: Every teacher in Edmonton must have trotted their kids through there.

Ernest Brown and Gladys Reeves.

GR: I think so. I remember the president of the chamber of commerce saying, "it would be a public tragedy to have the museum shut down." Didn't stop the government from kicking us out of our building when the war started. The government moved the contents of the museum from building to building, but by then the museum was a shadow of itself.

Alan: It's all he talked about when he came to visit, or when we met up for lunch.

GR: He worried constantly about the collection. More than was healthy.

Alan: I even came to help out on Saturdays, for a few months. I just didn't get it.

GR: Can't say I always did either. I saw their value, but he obsessed. He had a knack for shutting out the world when he was with the exhibits.

Alan: Mother used to dread the idea that she might end up with it if he died. Thank God he finally sold it all.

Scene 10: Government Sale, 1947

The living room of Ernest and Gladys's home, 1947. Ernest enters from the vestibule.

EB: *Shouting off stage.* This is all just a waste of my time. That's right—waste of time. I'm too important, and have more important things to be doing. Get out! Get out and don't come back!

GR: Ernest!

She exits to try to stop the man from leaving. A door slams.

EB: Pencil-pushing bureaucrat! Gladys! Bring me my tea.

GR: *Returns.* Well, he refused coffee, said he had to get home. How dare you treat Mr. MacDonald that way, after all he's trying to do for you!

EB: Do for me? Ha. Him and that "cultural activities branch."
        They wouldn't know real culture if it came and bit them
        in the . . .

GR: That's enough! The province has spent almost a year negoti-
        ating for your collection. It's a good deal. I know you want
        more, but enough is enough.

EB: I thought you were on my side.

GR: I am.

EB: How did they get to you, Gladys? Have they offered you a
        photography contract for the government? What aren't you
        telling me?

GR: Ernest, you're talking nonsense—

EB: What I have is a real piece of history. It's absolutely priceless.
        Why does no one understand that!!!

GR: Everyone understands. Or Mr. MacDonald would have
        given up this negotiation months ago.

EB: I don't want to sell.

GR: Why should you? You can just sit and stew here in my house,
        sifting and sifting through the collection day in and day out.

EB: I must get all of this straightened away before I'm gone.

GR: You're seventy, Ernest. You don't get to leave me yet. Damn
        you. You don't get to leave.

She shifts away.

EB: Gaga. You know that we'll be together again in the next life.

GR: Some comfort that is to me, halfway through this one.

An impasse.

GR: I don't want to see you sell either. But we need money. I can't take care of you and keep working at the pace I do.

EB: We are living in a province of infinite potential, Gladys. There is nothing we cannot accomplish. *If* we remember who we are, and what we have come from. Alberta is all drive forward, all sauce and sass. Our photos are essential to provide a kind of rudder. They point backward at our shared past so that we can move forward with aim and purpose.

GR: Calm down, Ernest. Don't get yourself agitated.

EB: Don't tell me to calm down.

GR: The front door sticks. The foundation is cracked, and the patch we put on the roof won't last more than a year. We can't afford to fix things properly, and we're on the verge of losing the house altogether. Then where will we store the collection, Ernest? Where?

EB: We won't lose the house. I won't let the City take another house from me.

GR: We're trying our best, but—

EB: Fine, I'll find a place if it comes to that.

GR: You barely leave the house any more. How could you possibly do that?

EB: Stop treating me like an invalid!

GR: Then take the province's money! Don't let them just wait you out, and simply scoop up the collection later. If you do this now, you have time to do it right, in an orderly manner, and you get some control over what happens to the negatives.

EB: I won't take less than fifty thousand dollars.

GR: You never know, he might come up a bit. Just be civil to him. Mr. MacDonald has a lot on his plate.

EB: Well, if he brings a bottle of scotch, it'll go a long way.

GR: I'll call him back in the morning.

EB: Single malt, mind you! None of that J&B stuff.

Scene 11: That Darn Plot

Transition to 1961.

GR: After a long year, he did reach an agreement with the government. Fifty thousand dollars for the lot. Quite a coup, really. I was so relieved. It was a stressful time—Ernest up and down depending on how each visit with Mr. MacDonald went.

Alan: Mother was astonished at the sum, but I thought he should have held out—

GR: Aren't you your father's son! But Ernest's health had been failing, and after the sale he seemed to fade even faster. That last year, I had to give up my studio to look after him.

Alan: I think Mother was relieved she didn't have to take care of him. Toward the end, he developed such an obsession with his collections.

GR: *With a small laugh.* It could be a little much. But those photos were the markers of our lives together.

Alan: It *has* been good to see you. Will you join us for the interment?

GR: Oh! I hadn't really thought about that.

Alan: Seventh Avenue cemetery.

GR: Same as your father.

Alan: Well, yes. She'll be next to him.

GR: What?

Alan: He did buy a double plot.

GR: I'd always thought I'd be buried with Ernest.

Alan: Oh!? I had no idea. I found the deed for the plot in Mother's things. They were still married, after all.

GR: But separated for thirty years.

Alan: They're my parents. And I'd like to see them together.

GR: Even after everything that happened between them? And me and Ernest?

Alan: It's what Mother wanted.

GR: Forty years means nothing. That's longer than they were together!

Alan: The plot was never yours.

GR: I devoted so much of my life to him, to his collections.

Alan: I did appreciate it. He will be remembered. A good part of that is thanks to you.

GR: Thanks to me? *This* is your thanks to me! Your father committed his life to a vision of brotherhood, compassion, honour. He would be ashamed of this. Ashamed of you.

She leaves with as much dignity as she can muster. Alan is silent for a moment. He pulls out a copy of Molly's will.

Alan: "I hereby bequeath to my son, Ernest Edward Alan Brown, my furniture and any other goods owned by me, Mary Brown. Also my late husband's roll top desk. Although it is at the home of Miss Gladys Reeves for storage until needed, it rightly belongs to my son."

One of the photos of Molly and Gladys together appears, and Alan approaches. Alan exits.

Scene 12: The Desk

Scene shifts to the next day. A doorbell. Slides shift to show a wall of framed photos, including photos of Ernest and Gladys. Gladys, perhaps in a dressing gown or other simple costume change, enters, shuffling a large handful of files and documents.

GR: Coming!

She exits. A brief offstage conversation is heard.

GR: Oh.

Alan: I'm sorry to intrude.

GR: I . . . No. Come in.

She leads him in. He has added a coat or something.

Alan: If this is a bad time.

GR: It's perfect. Tea?

Alan: No, thank you. I—

GR: Yesterday. I—I said a few things that I'd take back if I could. But I spent last night going over some of our old papers, and I think I may be able yet to convince you that I should be the one buried next to Ernest.

Alan: Gladys—

GR: Just hear me out! Now, you see this letter from him? It was from the Vegreville years, and he talks about how much strength and comfort he takes from me being "by his side." He even describes me as a "helpmeet." I think. His handwriting was especially appalling during that period. But the point is—

Alan: Gladys—

GR: And here! Here's an invitation we received in 1939, to dine with the deputy minister of . . . well, of something or other. Mr. Ernest Brown and Miss Gladys Reeves. The honour of our presence is requested. It might not always have been clear to people how to fit us into their world, but we found a way in life, and we could again in death. I mean, we're just lying there. How hard could it be?

Alan: Gladys, we buried Mother yesterday.

GR: *A pause. Possibly of some length. Possibly a dropping of the papers.* Oh. Oh, I see.

Alan bends to pick up papers.

Alan: I came to apologize.

GR: Leave the papers. I'll arrange them again later.

Alan: It's no trouble—

GR: No, there's an order I'll find for them. Really, you shouldn't bother yourself—

Alan: I don't mind—

GR: Don't touch them!

Alan puts down the papers and rises.

Alan: I apologize.

Gladys focuses on one of the photos framed on the wall.

GR: Do you see? I believe this is the last photo of Ernest. I made him my last sitting, before I closed down the business to take care of him.

Alan: Gladys, I never even thought . . . The men were already hired, the plot dug . . .

GR: Do you see—he still has that spark in his eye? You're too young to really remember him during his run for the labour party. He won more than a thousand votes in that election. He could speak fire for the mind and the heart. You can still see it here.

Alan: Gladys, do you happen to know a George Yoksima?

Heather D. Swain as Gladys Reeves and Mark Anderako as Ernest Brown, in the recreation of the Ernest Brown Photography Studio's darkroom at Fort Edmonton Park. Promotional photo for the original production, 2009.

NICOLE DIEBERT

GR: Ah . . . no, I don't believe so.

Alan: Mr. Yoksima has a double plot directly north of Father's. Buried ten years ago, and there's no Mrs. Yoksima there yet. I thought that perhaps we could make some inquiries about acquiring the plot . . .

GR: So that I could be . . . in the neighbourhood? *She considers it.* I think that after a lifetime of lying next to a man who's married to someone else, I should try something different in death.

Perhaps a shared laugh.

Alan: Is there something else I can . . .

GR: It occurs to me that it might better behoove me to live my next years to the fullest.

Alan: At least, then, I'd like to you keep Father's desk.

GR: His desk?

Alan: Yes. His roll top desk.

GR: I've had it since the thirties.

Alan: In any case, Mother thought it was hers. It was the only thing she specifically mentioned in her will, and that it was mine whenever I wanted it. But I'd like you to keep it.

GR: Well, thank you, I suppose. It does remind me of him, each time I sit down at it. I see the worn patch, where he'd tap his pen when he had writer's block. The stain, from the time I spilled the ink when I brought him tea. It's a map of the years we spent together.

Alan: And the initials.

GR: Initials?

Alan: Under the centre drawer. I saw them one day, when I was playing in Dad's study. "G R." They're not that obvious, but they're there.

GR: I'll have to look.

Alan: Goodbye then.

GR: Goodbye, Alan. *Shakes his hand.*

They pause and hug, a bit awkwardly. Alan starts to exit, and turns.

Alan: Perhaps I could come back some time? We could . . . look at photographs together?

GR: That would be lovely.

Alan exits. Gladys pulls out a photo. Looks at it. Turns it over and reads.

> The one I love dearest
> will leave me behind
> but will always be nearest
> and first in my mind.
> Tho' years may pass
> and time may seem dreary
> my love will last
> and never grow weary.

> Alan sure reminds me of you. Your firmness. Your voice.

Scene 13: Start Of The Affair

1911, or thereabouts. Gladys is looking around the darkroom. Ernest enters.

EB: Ah! Miss Reeves. Since business is picking up, and I need someone I can trust in the darkroom, it's time for you to learn how to develop photographs. You've been such as asset to me, and I think this will be a great challenge for you.

GR: *Very excited.* Yes, please! Ever since I started here, I've wanted to learn.

EB: Now. These chemicals help bring out the photograph. They need to be in this order, and for a precise amount of time. Developing the photographs is both a science and an art. I think you have the mind for it.

The first steps must be conducted in total darkness.

A lighting shift that suggests that Ernest has now turned off the lights.

You'll get used to it. I'll walk you through it. You know that the camera holds plates that are sensitive to the light.

GR: Yes, of course.

He hands her a box of glass slides, which she fumbles to hold.

EB: We'll start you out on the glass slides first. They're larger, and easier to work with.

EB steps in behind GR, and helps guide her hands to open up the box and remove a glass plate. Both are very aware of the proximity. They come to work in comfortable tandem.

GR: It's hard in the dark.

EB: You'll get used to it.

GR: It's all right to set the plate down?

EB: You lay it down, emulsion up, in this development bath.

GR: It smells like vinegar.

EB: You'll get used to it.

GR: Mrs. Brown always complains about the smell—

EB: You'll get used to it. Now, set the timer. Depending on the brightness of your initial exposure, about fifteen minutes should be right.

GR: Like this?

There is a moment of collision. Faces touch. It leads to a tentative first kiss that expands as the lights fade to black.

End

Beatrice Nasmyth at work in her London apartment.

FIRING LINES

JOURNALIST BEATRICE NASMYTH COVERS THE FIRST WORLD WAR

BY DEBBIE MARSHALL

Beatrice Nasmyth.

BEATRICE SIFTON NASMYTH

Beatrice Sifton Nasmyth was a reporter with Vancouver's *Daily Province* from 1910 to 1919. In 1914, the newspaper sent her to Britain to cover the First World War. Nasmyth was stationed in London, where she eventually became publicity secretary for the Alberta agent general. In 1917, she was campaign manager for Nursing Sister Roberta MacAdams. MacAdams ran successfully for a seat as a soldier's representative in the Alberta legislature, becoming one of the first two women elected to a legislature anywhere in what was then known as the British Empire. Before the war was over, Nasmyth would travel to France as a member of the first group of Canadian women journalists to tour the lines of communication. In 1919, Nasmyth covered the Versailles Peace Conference as press secretary to Canada's signatory, Arthur Sifton.

Firing Lines describes Nasmyth's experience as a war correspondent. It is adapted from the letters that the journalist sent home to her parents, along with some of the more than one hundred articles she wrote while overseas. The play also depicts a fictional encounter between fifty-four-year-old Nasmyth and thirty-four-year-old Second World War reporter Gladys Arnold. Arnold asks Nasmyth many of the questions that Debbie Marshall, the playwright, wishes she could have asked.

Firing Lines is dedicated to the late Monica Newton, Beatrice Nasmyth's daughter and Debbie Marshall's beloved friend.

Firing Lines was first produced by MAA and PAA Theatre and premiered at the Strathcona Library Theatre, Edmonton, Alberta, on August 17, 2011, with the following company:

Male characters*	Randy Brososky
Junior (Jr.) Bea	Jenny McKillop
Gladys Arnold	Jenny McKillop
Senior (Sr.) Bea	Heather D. Swain
other female characters**	Heather D. Swain

Director	David Cheoros
Sound and Set Design	Nicole Diebert
Costume Design	Geri Dittrich
Lighting Design	Gina Puntil

*Male characters include Guy Furniss, old man, sightseeing soldier, Lieutenant Charles Adams, man on street, Lieutenant Fred Sutton, Captain Gordon.

**Other female characters include Mary (a friend from the Alpine Ski Club), old woman, Christabel Pankhurst, Roberta MacAdams, Grace MacPherson.

The production ran approximately ninety minutes.

SET

To one side of the stage is a lectern with a sign saying "Canadian Women's Press Club AGM 1939" on the front. Two chairs sit on the opposite side of the stage. These will be moved about at various points in the play.

The following props are also used: small suitcase, tea trolley, tea pot, two cups and saucers, side plate, British flag, paper, pen, and a "painting" that acts as a screen on which slides were projected. In the original production, these slides were mainly chosen from the playwright's own collection, as well as from photographs provided by Monica Newton, Nasmyth's daughter.

COSTUMES

Jr. Bea/Gladys Arnold: A simple white blouse, below-the-knee dark skirt, dark shoes. A white, pinafore-style apron is added in scene 18. A heavy winter coat is worn in scene 30. Gladys Arnold wears glasses to differentiate her from Jr. Bea.

Sr. Bea/other women: Sr. Bea wears white gloves and a simple, tailored dress that extends below the knee. For other female characters, the following are used: a shawl for the role of the old woman (scene 6), a sash with "Join the Fight" written on it and an elaborate hat for the role of Miss Pankhurst (scene 16), a simple white head scarf as worn by Canadian nurses of the First World War for the role of Roberta MacAdams (scene 28), a winter coat, preferably leather, for the role of Grace MacPherson (scene 30).

Guy/other male characters: For military roles, a military uniform (circa 1914) is worn. In the original production, it was worn without a belt to allow for easy removal of jacket and transformation into other characters. Hat and jacket aren't worn when the actor is playing civilian roles. A great coat and duffle bag are used for the soldier in scene 18, a head bandage for Lieutenant Sutton (scene 22), a cane for Captain Gordon (scene 24), and a Glengarry cap for Guy Furniss (scene 26).

Middle-aged Beatrice Nasmyth, played by Heather D. Swain,
arguing with Gladys Arnold, played by Jenny McKillop.
DAVID CHEOROS

Scene 1: Canadian Women's Press Club, 1939

*Thirty-four-year-old Gladys Arnold rushes onto the stage with
a sheaf of papers in her hands. She is confident and "in charge."
Beside her is fifty-four-year-old Beatrice Nasmyth. Gladys is wearing
a simple blouse and below-the-knee dark skirt. Sr. Bea is immacu-
lately groomed, with hat and gloves, hat slightly askew—she is late
and is flustered.*

Sr. Bea: *Apologetic, upset.* I'm sorry I'm late. My son and I . . .

Gladys:	*Not really listening; perfunctory.* Don't worry. We're looking forward to your talk. Just to let you know, I'll be interrupting you from time to time to ask questions.
Sr. Bea:	Questions?
Gladys:	Yes, to make your talk more relevant to women today. You know, more up to date. After all, it's been *two decades* since you were in the war zone. *Sarcastic.* Things *have* changed . . .
Sr. Bea:	I see . . . *She seems distracted, not altogether there; her words seem to trail off.*
Gladys:	*Steps up to lectern, brisk, matter-of-fact.* Welcome to the annual general meeting of the Canadian Women's Press Club. I'm Gladys Arnold, the Paris correspondent for the Canadian Press. Tonight the world is at war. Our troops have been mobilized and are on their way to Britain. Given this state of affairs, our keynote speaker is especially appropriate. Some of our older members will remember her as Beatrice Nasmyth of the *Vancouver Province.* Beatrice was stationed in London during the last war, and was one of the first women journalists to visit the frontlines. Tonight she is going to tell us about her experience. *Steps away from podium.*
Sr. Bea:	*Gathers herself together, straightens her hat, steps up to podium; speaks very formally.* Thank you, Gladys. Twenty years ago, I prayed that we would never again find ourselves covering another European war. But sadly, we are being drawn into yet another dangerous conflict. Many of you, including Gladys, will have booked your passage overseas to cover the fight. It may be your first time as war correspondents. I was in that position in August 1914. I'd been a local journalist for five years. Then my editor at the *Province* told me that since war was likely between Britain and Germany, she wanted me on the spot in London.

The newspaper would cover my travel costs and buy every article I could send. But before I packed my bags, she gave me a piece of advice. "You are responsible, not only to me, but to your readers. When war comes, don't sacrifice the truth in the interests of patriotism." I barely listened. At that moment, all I could think about was getting overseas.

Scene 2: Off To London

Slide: interior of a train car, circa 1914.

SX: train sounds.

Young Bea is standing in the car of a train as it pulls out of the station. A suitcase sits beside her. As she turns back into the car, she sees a friend from the Alpine Ski Club. From Bea's movements, we can tell train is moving.

Jr. Bea: Mary! Off to the mountains again?

Mary: A bunch of us are hiking in Jasper. How about joining us?

Jr. Bea: *Regretfully.* I'd love to, but I can't. The *Province* is sending me to England, in case there's a war.

Guy: *He looks up from his newspaper.* There isn't going to be a war, you know. If there was, *I'd* know about it . . .

Jr. Bea: *She glances at Guy and back at Mary with a smile and raised eyebrow.* The King of England incognito!

Guy smiles and goes back to his paper. Jr. Bea steps forward, out of the scene, suitcase in hand, and addresses the audience.

The "King of England" was wrong. By the time our train reached Calgary, war had been declared. The Englishman who spoke to me on the train was vacationing in Canada. His name was Guy Furniss. We spent a lot of time together as our train crossed

Beatrice Nasmyth en route to Britain, 1914.
MONICA NEWTON COLLECTION

the Prairies. When we reached Halifax, I thought I'd never see him again. But when I boarded my ship for Britain, there was Guy, waiting on the deck. He'd booked a ticket on the same ship.

Slide: ship's deck, circa 1914.

Guy steps into the foreground, next to Jr. Bea. They turn toward one another.

Guy: I thought that if I was going home to join the army, I might as well enjoy the trip.

Jr. Bea: I guess being King of England does allow you *some* privileges!

Scene 3: Goodbye

SX: faint sound of waltz music while Sr. Bea is talking.

Guy and Jr. Bea dance a few steps.

Sr. Bea: The ship took a week to get to England. Guy and I spent every day together and danced every night until the band stopped playing. But we couldn't forget the war. As soon as it was dark, all lights on deck were put out to stop our ship from being torpedoed.

When we reached Liverpool, Guy left to join the army. He promised to write, but war makes promises harder to keep.

Guy lightly kisses Jr. Bea on the cheek and leaves the stage. She turns, picks up her suitcase, and steps forward, facing the audience.

Jr. Bea: I wanted to get to London. I would stay with friends until I got my bearings . . .

Scene 4: London

Slides: London street scenes and images of soldiers flow by.

SX: faint sound of "It's a Long Way to Tipperary."

Setting: interior of a London bus, circa 1914.

Jr. Bea: Anyone visiting London under military rule will find it a strange place. Traffic is constantly held up by long lines of British troops. They swing along, singing and whistling, companies of a thousand. Some in civilian clothes, others in uniform. As our bus drives past, we hear bits of songs. "The Marseillaise," "Rule Britannia," or that old favourite, "Tipperary." Khaki-coloured buses whiz past, driven by men in uniform. Some carry slogans like "Follow this for the Shortest Route to Germany" or "Khaki Express: Non-Stop to Berlin." Sometimes, a bandaged arm or leg protrudes

Postcard of London, England, in the first decade of the twentieth century.
AUTHOR'S COLLECTION

through the side coverings. The wounded brought home from the front. As they pass, people take off their hats in homage.

Then, of course, there are the Belgian refugees. There are nearly as many of them as there are soldiers. They wander the streets aimlessly, dressed in black.

We pass a vast park. Stretching in columns across the grassy field are thousands of recruits. We wait and watch while they are put through their exercises. Arms up, arms down, knees bent, knees straight. I wonder if they wouldn't stop a bullet just as easily without the strenuous preliminaries. Then the men drop on their stomachs and squirm away across the grass like a blanket of khaki-coloured lizards. Our driver laughs and says, "Strategic hadvance on the henemy, no doubt!"

Jr. Bea pulls a cord. There is a ringing bell or buzzer sound. She sways as though the bus is stopping, then "steps off" the bus, case in hand, walks over and stands by the two chairs at centre stage. She pretends to pull some knitting out of her case and begins to knit.

An elderly woman knitting, played by Heather D. Swain,
chats with an elderly man, played by Randy Brososky.
KAREN SIMONSON

Scene 5: Getting Started

Sr. Bea: Life in London wasn't as easy as I imagined it would
be. Since my newspaper was only paying me by the
story, I had to find a full-time job to support me.
Until things fell into place, I did what every woman
seemed to be doing—I knitted socks for soldiers.

*She puts on a shawl, becomes an old woman, walks over and sits down
at one of the chairs near Jr. Bea. See end of scene 4. Then she begins
to expertly "knit" a half-finished sock. An elderly man enters and sits
at the chair opposite her. He is holding a half-full whisky glass. Jr. Bea
stands in the middle, just behind the pair. She is "knitting," but is
having a difficult time of it.*

Scene 6: Knitting

Jr. Bea: *Throws down her knitting in disgust.* I'll never get the hang of this!

Old woman: *Old woman looks up from her knitting, startled. English accent, upper class.* You must be from "Canadaw!"

Jr. Bea: *Smiles.* Yes, Vancouver, actually.

Old woman: I understand that you Canadians have sent over a troop of wild Indians to fight the "Ki-zar!"

Jr. Bea: *A slight pause, looks amused and slightly mischievous, then takes a serious tone.* Quite true, Madame. I arrived in Liverpool just last week. The first flotilla of war canoes overtook our ship a few hours before we docked. The war whoop of the painted savages as they bore down on us, mistaking us for the enemy, was blood-curdling. I tremble to think of its effect on the Kaiser!

Old man: *English accent, upper class.* Indeed! I'm not surprised! I know quite a bit about your country, you know . . .

Jr. Bea: Really?

Old man: Oh yes! My maiden aunts live there and they've written to me about your strange burial practices.

Jr. Bea: *A little wary.* Burial practices?

Old woman: *Very curious.* What *do* they *do*?

Old man: *As though taking everyone into his confidence. Old woman looks on intently.* It's most peculiar. When a man dies, they dress him up in his best suit, as though he were still alive. Then they paint his face, color his lips, tint his hands, and make him look as life-like as possible. Then he is placed in a chair and receives the mourners. They come in and shake hands with him, tell him how well he's looking, wish him a pleasant journey and all that. After that, he's taken to the cemetery and put on a shelf until spring. When spring comes they have the real funeral and he is buried properly. Most peculiar, isn't it? My maiden aunts told me all about it!

Jr. Bea: *Trying to be calm.* Where do they live?

Old man: *Slight pause.* In Toronto.

Jr. Bea: *Opting for diplomacy.* I haven't lived in Toronto for years. Since then I've been living in the wildest part of the country—Vancouver, Edmonton, and Calgary—and of course, customs vary.

Old man: Of course. In the parts you speak of, the dead are buried in totem poles. But in Toronto, no one can be buried without the reception. I wish you could meet my maiden aunts. They could tell you the most interesting things.

Jr. Bea: *Firmly.* I don't doubt it.

She walks across the stage and becomes Gladys.

Scene 7: Socks

Sr. Bea: *At lectern. Bemused.* I felt sorry for the soldier who got the socks I made that day. Knitters were everywhere—on street corners, in restaurants, even on buses . . .

Gladys: Excuse me, Beatrice. I'm sure that the women here are more interested in your war experiences than in your knitting.

Sr. Bea: *Startled, then drily, looking directly at Gladys.* I suppose socks don't have much to do with war. But the men in the trenches went through them quickly enough.

Gladys walks over to the chair on stage to become Jr. Bea.

I finally got a chance to report on our side of the war in late October. That's when the first wave of Canadians arrived in England. There were over thirty thousand, all young and green. The British thought they weren't battle-ready, so they were sent for training. I wrote about those new recruits in a story called . . .

Scene 8: First Story

Slide: bed-sitting room.

Sr. Bea & Jr. Bea: *In unison.* "Canadian Soldier Lads See World's Metropolis."

SX: "Maple Leaf Forever" to be played softly under the monologue.

Jr. Bea pulls the "sheet" out of the typewriter and reads her news story aloud; very upbeat, patriotic, and optimistic. As she reads, a Canadian soldier enters the stage with a guidebook in his hands. He walks around, as though a tourist looking at the sights. Sr. Bea may also pretend to be a civilian on the street, bemused by the unfamiliar sight of the Canadian soldier.

Slides: photos of London sights, circa 1914.

Jr. Bea: November 7, 1914. The khaki-clad Canadian has come to London to see the sights. And to the Canadian abroad, he looks taller and straighter and more efficient than any of the other soldiers which throng the metropolis. Up from his huge camp at Salisbury Plain he comes with a cheerful air. He flits about in taxis, he parades the streets. He threads through traffic and puts a dozen questions to the policeman. He even penetrates to the churches, galleries, and museums. Yet, for the most part, he is most comfortable in the upper seats of a double-decker bus. From this elevation he views the scene about him with the frankest interest.

One learns to look for the six raised letters which spell Canada. One wonders, too, what these men will face after their sightseeing is over and they are sent to join the struggle for peace and freedom.

Prophecies about what is to be done with the Canadian troops vary widely. One man says they will eat Christmas dinner either on Salisbury Plain or en route home again. The next says that they will be at the front within three weeks. However, one thing is certain. In whatever form our Canadians serve their country, they will bring credit to King and Empire.

SX: "Maple Leaf Forever" that gets louder and louder as Jr. Bea transforms herself into Gladys and steps forward to talk to Sr. Bea.

Scene 9: Censorship

Slide: soggy-looking Canadian soldiers on Salisbury Plain.

Gladys: My uncle was stationed at Salisbury Plain. His best friend died of meningitis. It was one of the coldest winters and they were living in tents! While they waited, eighty thousand British soldiers were wounded or dying in France. Why weren't those facts in your story?

Sr. Bea: *Angry in a controlled and refined sort of way.* Most of us didn't know what was really going on. Journalists were banned from France—anyone at the front without military permission could be shot as a spy. Even when we were allowed into the war zone, it was impossible to report the whole story. There were censors at all telegraph stations—

Gladys: *Interrupts.* If censorship was so tough, why bother covering the war?

Sr. Bea: I was writing as much of the truth as I could.

Gladys:	Wouldn't it have been better to tell the real story about what the men were facing? You made it sound like a holiday—
Sr. Bea:	At the beginning, the war was a big adventure. Most soldiers had never been out of their hometowns, never mind overseas. And they wanted to right some wrongs. Do you know about the atrocities in Belgium? The German army massacred innocent men, women, and children. When Canada was asked to defend her allies, our men went willingly and they were ready to fight. *Pause.* Now I'd like to ask you a question.
Gladys:	*Surprised.* Go ahead.
Sr. Bea:	Why are you returning to Paris? I imagine you'll get censored, too. Why bother to cover the war if you can't tell all of it?
Gladys:	*Caught off guard, angry, vehement.* We have to try to let people know what Hitler's doing. As if Spain, Czechoslovakia, and Poland weren't enough. He'll march into France unless he's stopped . . .
Sr. Bea:	*Stalemate.* I guess times haven't changed so much then . . .

They glare at one another. Then Gladys steps back into role of Jr. Bea while Sr. Bea continues talking.

Sr. Bea:	*Serious, addressing the audience now.* By 1915, we knew the war was going to be a long and brutal affair. Two lines of trenches stretched across Belgium and France. In between was a wasteland filled with muddy corpses— hundreds of thousands of French and German soldiers, not to mention most of Britain's best soldiers. But that didn't stop thousands more from volunteering to fill dead men's shoes. Our Canadians got to France in March. *Change mood, more upbeat.* As for me, I finally had a paying job to support me while I wrote their stories . . .

Scene 10: The Canadian Pay And Records Office

Slide: portrait of King George V. Jr. Bea pushes the tea trolley into the centre of the stage. Trolley has a tea pot, cup, saucer, and plate on it. Canadian officer—he should look slightly disreputable—enters and sits down, reading through a pile of papers. Jr. Bea is pouring a cup of tea. Officer comes around the desk as she is bending over the trolley.

Officer: Can I help you with that?

He leans over her from behind, puts his hand over hers as she lifts the plate of cookies. His other arm encircles her waist and he holds her tightly.

Jr. Bea: *Icily; struggles out of his grip.* Let me go, if you don't mind.

Officer: I do mind. Have you reconsidered—

Jr. Bea: *Very angry, extricates herself, definite. Picks up cup and saucer.* I'm not interested . . .

Officer: *Joking.* I thought women were supposed to comfort the troops—

Jr. Bea: *Quick, angry, sarcastic.* I'm shocked. I didn't know we were to serve the war effort by lying back and thinking of England.

Officer: *Mood change, angry, menacing, stepping toward her.* That is not the kind of comment I'd expect from a woman like you.

Jr. Bea: Women like me aren't attracted to men like you. I'm writing a letter to your superior officer. If you continue, I'll mail it.

Officer: Do you think he'll believe you?

He smiles and advances on her again. She empties the cup of tea on his shirt. He steps back and then wipes his shirt. He starts to walk away, but turns briefly.

You'll change your mind. *Exits.*

Bea, struggling to regain her composure, picks up a pen and a letter to her father from the trolley and jots a few words.

Jr. Bea: Dear Dad. It's hard to believe, but it's been three weeks since I started my new job at the Canadian Pay and Records Office. Over seven hundred soldiers work here. Most were at the front and are now unfit to return. The office also employs one hundred civilians and I am the only woman among them. I work in the department that looks after the estates of dead soldiers. I write letters and reports and look after the tea trolley. Unfortunately, all the Canadian men confide in me, from the corporal who tells me about his barroom brawls, to the lieutenant who doesn't want to be sent back to the trenches and describes his experiences with tears in his eyes and touching references to his wife and child. Then there is the Edmonton officer who takes every opportunity to pin me into a corner. And they all want to get back to Canada.

There is one soldier I do like. He's a Toronto boy who just returned from a French hospital. He's pale and coughs a lot, but he's got a good sense of humour. Around here they call him "The Night Before Christmas." He sits all day long at a huge table and makes up little bundles, just like we used to do on Christmas Eve. Some contain an old cigarette tin, blood-stained letters, odd-shaped stones, twisted bullets, or foreign coins. Others hold rosaries and photographs. They're the things found on the bodies of dead soldiers. When they are bundled up, they are sent home to the dead men's families.

Anyhow, my filing won't wait and I've got more tea to serve. Send me copies of any of my articles that appear in the *Province*. All my love, Beatrice.

Scene 11: Confrontation

Sr. Bea: *At lectern; as though coming back to the present abruptly.* I didn't tell my dad everything about the records office. I was often propositioned, usually by married men. Since the war demanded their lives, they thought they could demand our bodies.

Gladys: They must have got the idea from somewhere.

Sr. Bea: *Surprised, shocked.* Don't tell me your generation believes that when a woman receives unwanted male attention, she must have invited it.

Gladys: If the shoe fits . . .

Sr. Bea: *Icy, angry.* It doesn't.

Gladys: Surely war makes independent women more open to . . . romance. You wouldn't be the first to fall for a uniform.

Sr. Bea: In those days, I never "fell" for anyone I didn't choose freely. Life was too short. Soon after I began at the records office, the Germans began to bomb London.

Gladys: They're still bombing civilians . . .

Sr. Bea: At night, women and children slept in underground stations. I once counted eighty-seven children under four, all set out in rows. Other people hid in basements. But some didn't bother to hide at all when the raids began.

Scene 12: Zeppelin

Slide: Jr. Bea's bed-sitting room. Jr. Bea is sleeping.

Sr. Bea: One Tuesday night I awoke from what some optimists called a "beauty sleep." Subconsciously I had been hearing distant reverberations, each a little different from the thousand other night noises of the city.

SX: loud explosion.

Jr. Bea falls out of bed as though shot out of a cannon.

Jr. Bea: Zepps!

She gets up and lurches over to the "window" and "opens" it. While she is doing this, Sr. Bea continues to read.

Sr. Bea: I remembered standing two days earlier in front of one of the big windows in a shop on Oxford Street. The window was furnished as a bedroom. At the head of the bed, a table was topped with a flashlight, a clock, and smelling salts. A fire extinguisher was nearby. On the floor were a pair of slippers and a pail of water. The viewer is given two guesses as to where a panic-stricken civilian would put his feet first. An elegant dressing gown was draped over a chair. Now I was to have a "window display" all to myself.

Jr. Bea leans out of her "window."

Lighting: search lights light up the room, criss-crossing.

SX: distant sounds of crashing bombs, anti-aircraft fire, and the faint sound of breaking glass.

Sr. Bea: The firing of the anti-aircraft guns fascinated me. I found myself counting the explosions. Somewhere up in the great expanse of night were hostile airships. It is difficult to convey the sensation of absolute vulnerability one feels when bombs are dropping on all sides.

There is a lull, no bomb sounds or anti-aircraft; Jr. Bea continues to look outside.

Remembering it all afterward, it never once occurred to me that a bomb might drop in my vicinity. I was at the window less than ten minutes. Then the noise stopped and it dawned on me that I was getting cold from standing in the window in my nightgown.

She moves to the front of the stage as though outside and looks skyward. Man comes on stage and stands there, looking around as though he has also just come out of his house.

Sr. Bea: I joined my housemates on the sidewalk. The Zeppelins seemed to have passed over and gradually the explosions grew more distant. Then I looked around me.

Jr. Bea and the man look around and at each other.

It was clear that no one had seen the air raid display on Oxford Street. No one was wearing a respirator or using smelling salts. The gowns and slippers were not very fashionable and in a few cases were missing altogether!

Scene 13: Avoiding The Censor

Sr. Bea: The government tried to suppress the news of the air raid. They were afraid it would turn the public against the war effort. But seventy-one people had been killed. Canadians needed to know what had happened. Since the mail and telegraph were being censored, I used a courier. My brother was in London on business. When he went home, he hand-delivered my article to the *Province*. They ran it *uncut*. By then, I was finding stories everywhere.

Scene 14: Introducing Lieutenant Adams

Slide: room decorated for Christmas.

SX: dance music, perhaps "Roses of Picardy," played as though for dancing.

Jr. Bea is almost finished a dance with a young Canadian soldier—it's obvious they are attracted to one another. The music ends. They stop to talk.

Jr. Bea: You promised me an interview in exchange for that dance!

Jenny McKillop as a young Beatrice Nasmyth dancing
with Lt. Charles Adams, played by Randy Brososky.

Adams: I know. But the moon is full, the night is young, and
I thought . . .

Jr. Bea: I know what you thought. For now, let's at least get
this interview done. I'll make it as painless as possible.

Adams: What do you want to know?

Jr. Bea: *Smiling.* How about name, rank, and regiment . . .

Adams:	*Saluting.* Lieutenant Charles Cecil Ogden Adams, 16th Canadian Scottish, at your service.
Jr. Bea:	*Flirting, mischievous.* All right, Lieutenant Adams, why don't you begin by describing life in the trenches . . .
Adams:	*Seriously.* Do you really want to know?
Jr. Bea:	*Serious now.* Yes, I do.
Adams:	*Starts out steady, but as he continues, his voice sometimes shakes.* A week ago, my men and I were ordered to take a German trench. Shrapnel was flying and it seemed like suicide. We pushed through the mud and noise. Some of my men were killed, but at last we managed to take the trench. It was filled with dead Canadians and Germans. Since we had to spend the night there, we piled the bodies in corners so we could get some sleep. The next day we were pinned down under a terrific bombardment. We couldn't move—men were screaming and dying all around us.

From the whizzing overhead and the sound of the bursting I could calculate the distance between our section of the trench and the place where the shells were landing. I began to realize that each shell was coming a few yards closer with each shot. There was nothing I could do but sit and wait and count, wondering if the next one would . . . *He stops, as though unable to cope with the memory.*

When it was all over and we climbed out of that hole in the ground, I didn't feel anything. It was as though I'd been turned into something cold sitting in that trench. I should have been overjoyed—after all, we'd survived, while other battalions had lost hundreds of men. I was all right until the next night. I had sent some men out to raid the German trenches. On their way back, our sentries mistook them for Germans and shot them dead.

Beatrice Nasmyth's passport photo.

Postcard of Trafalgar Square, London, during the First World War.

Jr. Bea: That's awful. *Sympathetically.* You've witnessed terrible things . . .

Adams: When my sergeant told me the news, it was as though I'd lost my own brother. Something in me collapsed. I passed out and when I woke up, I couldn't speak. I ended up in hospital for weeks. *Silence; then abruptly.* But I got over it. They had that new electric shock treatment. It's amazing how quickly words come back when you've had a few volts of electricity applied to your throat.

Jr. Bea: *Gently taking his hands in hers.* I think we've talked enough about the war for now, don't you?

Adams: *Comes back to the present and meets her eyes.* Definitely. How about another dance?

He stands up, holds out his hands and then whirls Bea into a dance.

SX: Song played in a bouncy dance tempo, perhaps "Your King and Country Want You."

Scene 15: Confrontation

Slide: photo of Bea wearing brooch.

Sr. Bea: We spent every night together until the end of Charles's leave. He gave me one of his badges and told me that next time he was in London, he'd collect it personally.

Gladys: *Drily.* That was one romance that you seem to have "chosen freely."

Sr. Bea: I suppose it was.

Gladys: Too bad it affected your professionalism.

Sr. Bea: *Affronted.* What do you mean?

Gladys: I read your article about Lieutenant Adams. You didn't mention that he had shell shock and had to be hospitalized. Instead you just made him sound like a hero.

Sr. Bea: *Embarrassed.* He was a hero. It would have been wrong to portray him as . . .

Gladys: Cowardly?

Sr. Bea: Vulnerable.

Gladys: Forgive me. I didn't know that the objective of journalism was to make weak men look strong . . .

Sr. Bea: Around the time that Charles returned to the front, I quit my job at the Pay and Records Office. I'd been offered a public relations job at the Alberta agent general's office in London. I was soon in charge of promoting all things Albertan—from crops to settlement.

Scene 16: A New Job

Slide: Trafalgar Square.

Jr. Bea is sitting behind her office desk, reading over a letter to her father.

Jr. Bea: Dear Dad. I came into the office early this morning so that I could write you about my new job as publicity secretary. My office is on the fourth floor of a building that overlooks Trafalgar Square. Since I'm supposed to be promoting immigration to Alberta, I've been kept busy learning as much about the province as I can. For instance, yesterday a man called for information about Bottle Ridge. I spent the morning finding it on a map, the kind of people who had settled there, the amount of rainfall, the condition of the land, etc., etc. This deluded me into thinking I'd be ready when a similar question came in. But one never did—the next person wanted to know the address of the official dog catcher in Bog Gulch, and the third whether his third cousin who lived in Lethbridge had died with or without a will. It never gets monotonous around here.

She walks over to the "window" and looks out, still holding her letter.

During the few times that I do get a free minute or two, and that's not often, I look out my window to see what's happening in Trafalgar Square. I've got a great view, Dad. All very bright and colourful. Uniformed women are everywhere—from bus conductors in their smart black outfits to munitions workers in their canary yellow uniforms rushing off to work. Three giant orange banners have been hung on the front of the National Gallery. One says "Our Food Supplies are Low." Another says "Will Germany Starve Us?" while the third answers the question with "We Must Grow More Food."

Do you remember the speeches I once gave for women's rights? Today, a group of suffragettes are holding a recruiting meeting by Nelson's Column. They've got signs, too. "If You Can't Fight for Your Country, Work for It" and "England Needs the Best that Every Man Can Do for Her Today." There's Miss Pankhurst, all ready to give a speech. I wish you were here to see it all, Dad. All my love, Beatrice.

She continues to look with interest out of the window. At this point Sr. Bea transforms herself into a suffragette—Christabel Pankhurst—and steps to the front of the stage. Pankhurst is wearing an elaborate hat and a sash across her chest saying "Join the Fight!"

Slides: men enlisting, women doing war work.

Pankhurst: *British aristocratic accent.* We suffragettes have temporarily given up our struggle for the vote in order to come to the aid of our country. Britain is fighting for her national existence and for the principles of freedom and self-government. Germany hacked her way through Belgium to France. She is hacking her way through France to Britain—if she can get here. If we, as women, are to enjoy equality one day, we must stop Germany from destroying the country whose citizenship we most desire. You who are gathered here must do what you can to help our nation. If you are a man and can fight, join your brothers in the trenches. If you are a woman, take a man's job so that he can go to the front. Make the munitions that will turn the tide of this war for freedom. Our nation depends on you.

Scene 17: Women In Men's Shoes

She takes off her sash and hat and returns to the lectern as Sr. Bea.

Sr. Bea: By the end of 1916, a million and a half British soldiers were dead. Any hope for a clear-cut victory had been abandoned. The need for troops was so pressing that Britain introduced conscription. All able-bodied women had to take men's jobs so they would be freed to join the military. Suddenly there were women welders, bank tellers, and munitions workers. Many fed the soldiers in clubs and canteens. As a staunch suffragette, I wondered what it was like for those who volunteered to help our fighting men. In January 1916, I got a chance to find out.

Scene 18: Charing Cross Station

Slide: a sign saying "Free Buffet for Soldiers and Sailors." Then the slide is changed to an image of an old-fashioned train station clock.

SX: sound of steam trains, steam, occasional whistles.

Jr. Bea wears a white bibbed apron over her clothes. She's at Charing Cross Station. Behind her is her trolley, draped in a British flag. On top of the trolley is a tea pot, cups, and plate.

Jr. Bea: *Addressing the audience like an old friend.* The station buffet for soldiers and sailors has become almost as much a British institution as the "ipe-ney bun." *Pronounced "hape-knee."* In all the big London stations are free stalls where the travelling Tommy may refresh himself with a mug of coffee and a sandwich. It takes a large corps of volunteers to manage the booths and serve the steady stream of men who patronize them. Tonight I've been given the opportunity to be one of those volunteers.

Picture for yourself a huge glass-arched station with a dozen rows of tracks. Imagine the smell of soft coal and ancient waiting-rooms. Pretend that the sound in your ears is the constant booming, echoing, clanging, and reverberations of a great railway junction. And if your imagination holds out this far, button your coat against the cold drafts that blow under the arches from one end of the station to the other.

Heather D. Swain as Christabel Pankhurst, giving a speech.

And now, if you are still in an imaginative mood, conjure up a mental picture of yourself dressed in a blue uniform as you stand behind the station buffet at this big junction. You have been waiting for thirty minutes in the dim half-light of the station. The atmosphere is cold and grey. Just as you are beginning to wonder when things are going to start happening, there is a roar and a boom. A long troop train rushes into the station and comes to a standstill on the main track just across the first platform from the buffet.

Clanging of doors, hiss of steam, whistle; Beatrice strains and looks forward, half horrified.

As the doors fly open you think of a disturbed hornets' nest, for a khaki swarm pours from every opening and you see the cloud of them coming straight toward you.

Jr. Bea acts as though she is handing out food and coffee to many soldiers. A soldier enters, carrying a khaki duffle bag over his shoulder. He looks tired and disheveled. There is a streak of mud on his face. He struggles to get through the "crowd" to Jr. Bea. He takes the mug she offers and pretends to wolf down some food.

Soldier: Thanks. Haven't had anything but bully beef since I left the trenches.

Jr. Bea: You've got some mud on your face . . . Didn't you have time to clean up before you left France?

Soldier: *His mouth is full.* Didn't want to stop. Had to catch the first troop ship. As long as you're in France they can cancel your leave any time, especially if there's a big push. This is my first trip home since 1914.

Jr. Bea: *Slowing down, as though there are fewer people to serve.* What's the first thing you'll do when you get home?

Soldier: *Looks slightly baffled.* You mean after I've kissed my wife and . . . Never mind. *Slowly.* Well, I'm going to sit in a hot bath for as long as it takes to clean off the smell of sweat and blood and death. I'm going to introduce myself to my son—he was born a few months after I left—and then I'm going to . . .

SX: A train whistle sounds.

That's my train 'ome. Goodbye, sweetheart. *Shouts back.* Any messages for the Kaiser when I get back to the front? *He exits quickly.*

Jr. Bea: *Looks torn.* Yes, but I don't think he'd listen . . .

Scene 19: A "Happy" War

Sr. Bea: *Reflecting back with a sense of satisfaction.* My story on the station buffet ran as a half-page feature, entitled "Penny Buns and Coffee: How Some of the Women of London Supply Comforts to the Soldiers." I was writing two in-depth stories every month, sometimes more.

Gladys: Sounds like your war was a happy one.

Sr. Bea: *Surprised.* What do you mean?

Gladys: You benefited from the war. Since most of the men were away, women journalists like you were in demand. There were exciting stories to write, you weren't being shot at, and you had lots of material for your stories.

Sr. Bea: *Angry.* What would you know about what it was like to live in the shadow of war?

Gladys: *Vehement.* I reported on the Spanish Civil War. Many of my friends and comrades died fighting Franco. You don't seem to have paid much of a price for your work.

Sr. Bea: *Bemused, ironic.* Then I suppose all the women who did "safe" war work could be accused of the same thing—enjoying steady work and steady pay while the men suffered. Mind you, it might be hard to convince the factory girls who died of TNT poisoning, or the ones who got lung cancer after the war.

Gladys:	I'm not speaking of them; I'm speaking about you as a journalist. I just think you gained a lot and didn't suffer much.
Bea:	Suffering is a personal matter, isn't it? Easy to measure for others but always a little harder to measure for yourself. In those days, almost everyone had someone they cared about fighting in France. To say that the war was a great time for any woman, no matter her job, is offensive when you consider how many had loved ones who were killed, returned home blinded, with amputated limbs or shell-shocked minds. You were only a step away from grief . . .

Scene 20: "We Don't Want To Lose You"

Slide: bed-sitting room.

SX: faint playing of "Your King and Country Want You" or other suitable First World War song in the background and gradually fading out.

Gladys steps back into her role as Jr. Bea. She is sitting at her desk in her bedroom, holding a typed article and a red pencil. In this scene, Jr. Bea and Sr. Bea will be speaking—Jr. Bea in her bedroom, Sr. Bea from the lectern.

Jr. Bea:	*Reading her story aloud, as though she can hardly speak.* London, July 16, 1916. "How Lieutenant Adams Fell in Battle." *Pause.* A few days ago I talked with a comrade of the late Lieutenant Adams during the last few weeks in the life of that gallant young Vancouver officer. It reminded me of the last time I had seen Lieutenant Adams in London. The news that he had made the supreme sacrifice was hard to accept. He was so tremendously alive when I saw him last.
Sr. Bea:	*Remembering.* So alive . . .

Randy Brososky as Lt. Charles Adams.
KAREN SIMONSON

Jr. Bea: Lieutenant Adams's relatives and friends have been told something of the way in which he died. His life was laid down as bravely as it was lived. Those who were with him in the long struggle, and just before his death, speak with a sorrow that glows with admiration and regret. His superior officer has said that had he lived, he would have been recommended for decoration and properly rewarded.

Sr. Bea: They always told the bereaved that their loved ones died quickly and bravely, as though that would take away the pain of their loss . . .

Lt. Adams enters the stage. He stands at attention. The women do not see him. A bright light shines on Adams.

Jr. Bea: For some months before his death, Lieutenant Adams was attached to the intelligence department. His confidence in the face of danger enabled him to root out valuable information. His bravery inspired his men to follow him at all times.

Lt. Adams looks around, as though ferreting out information. He pretends to write things down, hands the information to "others." Jr. Bea takes out her red pencil and crosses something out and appears to write in something else.

Sr. Bea: His daring masked his fear and exhaustion. When he could sleep at all, the dead appeared in his dreams and he woke up shouting. *Adams looks frightened, anxious, as though waking from terrible dreams.*

Jr. Bea: *Reading from her article.* Some weeks before the last charge, Lieutenant Adams was struck in the neck by a piece of shrapnel. When taken to hospital, he was suffering from shell shock. *She stumbles in her words and then collects herself.* Adams became impatient to return to the front and left the hospital sooner than he should have done. "I must carry on," he said. *Adams stands tall, brave.*

Sr. Bea:	*Almost angry.* Charles was ashamed. He believed he had failed his men. He returned to his regiment just as they were going into battle. *Adams does the actions as though he is in the midst of battle.* The Canadians were holding a hill called Mount Sorrel and a crest of land called Observatory Ridge. The Germans bombarded them, day and night. The shelling was so intense that entire trenches were destroyed. Trees, weapons, and bodies were thrown up into the air. Then the enemy poured down on our men like waves crashing on a beach. Observatory Ridge was lost and the Germans had the upper hand.
Jr. Bea:	*Reading, stumbling; this is difficult.* News came that the Canadians were to charge the enemy and retake all the ground that had been lost. The attack began at dawn. As the Canadian artillery roared, Lieutenant Adams and his men emerged from the mud and began to move forward. Just as they regained Observatory Ridge, a high explosive shell killed Lieutenant Adams. *She breaks down.*

Adams stands very still. He looks over at Jr. Bea longingly, then exits the stage.

SX: sound of "Your King and Country Want You," played cheerfully; starts quietly and gets louder and louder . . .

Scene 21: Recovery

Sr. Bea:	*Detached.* I was told that he was buried in a lovely little cemetery behind the lines. It was a comforting lie. High explosive shells don't leave much behind. *She glances at Gladys.* I told his story straight that time.
Gladys:	What did you do after he died?
Sr. Bea:	When you lost someone you loved during the war, you couldn't grieve for long. Others were in the same

boat, and pining didn't bring the men back from the dead. Besides, you had to think of the living. So many young men are risking their lives and they need our support. I mean, *were* risking their lives. *She stops for a moment, as though it is hard to continue; then focuses.*

Many journalists spent time visiting the wounded; it was a way to help the war effort while gathering first-hand accounts of what was happening in the war zone.

Scene 22: Lieutenant Sutton

Slide: military hospital ward. Soldier with bandaged forehead is sitting on a chair.

Jr. Bea: It's good to meet you, Lieutenant Sutton.

Sutton: Call me Fred.

Jr. Bea: Well then, call me Beatrice. I'm from Vancouver. I hear that you're a westerner, too.

Sutton: Sure am. I was prospecting in the Peace River country when the war began. I went to Edmonton right away and joined the 49th Battalion. I'd flown before, but had to get to England before I could transfer into the Royal Flying Corps.

Jr. Bea: I hear that loads of Canadians are in the RFC.

Sutton: There ought to be a Canadian Flying Corps. Forty per cent of the Royal Flying Corps are Canadians, and they're making good, too.

Jr. Bea: How did you end up here?

Sutton: *Acts out the story as he tells it, sometimes incorporating Jr. Bea into the role of Jimmie Ross.* It happened in July, during the first two days of the big push. On the

Lt. Sutton, daredevil pilot of the First World War.
BERNIE QUIGLEY

first day, we were in the air before daylight, watching the advance of the British. I was at the front of the plane in the observer's seat, operating the wireless and manning our gun. My pal Jimmie Ross was the pilot.

We were under fire from German planes, anti-aircraft fire from the ground, and flying shrapnel from our own shells. Our plane was shot through in eight places. We saw German howitzers pointing at us, their noses gleaming in the sun. Just one shell from them would have blown us to pieces. Yet luck was with us. One actually flew between our planes and left us unscathed.

Jr. Bea: They say that flying is the riskiest wartime profession.

Sutton: I'm not so sure. The men in the trenches haven't a chance in the world. From the sky, they seem so weak and small and their battles look so cruel and futile. When they advance, they look like long rows of tiny sandbags moving across the open plain. Then come white puffs of smoke from enemy guns and you see arms and legs fly out from the sandbags and you know they were once men.

Jr. Bea: When did things start to go wrong for you?

Sutton: On the second afternoon, when one of our guns was knocked out by a shell. A German plane was flying just below us, in a good position for a shot. I turned the other gun on it, but before I could fire, the nose of our gun was shot away. I looked back to signal Jimmie. He was hanging over the edge of the plane! He was unconscious. His arm was twisted into a gruesome shape and dangling over the side. Our plane was drifting toward the German lines!

Jr. Bea: Good heavens. What did you do next?

Sutton: Just as I took in this pretty situation—*he looks at Jr. Bea flirtatiously*—a bullet caught me in the hip. For a few moments I lost consciousness. I think it was another dose of shrapnel in the head that brought me to. I was covered with blood. Bullets were spraying our plane like a hailstorm.

I managed to crawl back into the pilot's seat. I had to sit on Jimmie's knee to land the machine. *He attempts to sit on Jr. Bea's knee, but she pushes him off with a smile.* Although we were on the British side, our troubles weren't over. Our plane was resting on a low hill in range of German fire. I was going to try carrying Jimmie to safety when help came.

Some British Tommies pulled our plane down into a hollow. Jimmie and I were sent to hospital. He'll have a badly crippled arm, but nothing but luck came my way. Just look at me. I'll be back at the front before you know it.

Jr. Bea: You seem to lead a charmed life. Do you always feel confident you'll return?

Sutton: *Serious.* Quite the opposite. We never really expect to land safely once we go up in the air—we just hope our luck will hold out. But that risk is as much a part of flying as filling our gas tanks.

When appropriate, Jr. Bea steps forward into her role as Gladys.

Scene 23: Journalism

Sr. Bea: Flying was a risky business. Survivors like Fred Sutton were rare. Most pilots only lasted three weeks. Those who weren't killed or wounded had breakdowns.

Gladys: Sutton seemed sane enough. He enjoyed being interviewed.

Sr. Bea: Most of the men were proud of what they were doing and were pleased that others were interested. Some gilded the lily a little. I later found out that Fred Sutton didn't fly the plane down—Jimmie Ross did, just before he lost consciousness. But for the most part, his story was true.

Gladys: Did you ever interview someone you didn't like?

Sr. Bea: *Slowly, thinking back.* A few times. I especially remember an interview with a British officer on a bench at Hyde Park.

Scene 24: Encounter At Hyde Park

Slide: trees, park-like setting.

Gladys becomes Jr. Bea and walks over to the two chairs at centre stage. A British officer is standing in front of the two chairs at centre stage. He is using a cane.

Jr. Bea: Captain Gordon. *She extends her hand to shake his.* I'm so glad you're willing to speak with me. I know that when soldiers are on leave, they want to do anything but talk about their life in France.

Gordon: *Formal.* It would have been ungallant to turn you down. Please join me. *She sits down first and then he sits beside her.* What can I tell you?

He stops and puts his hand to his ear and shakes his head slightly, as though to soothe a temporary irritation.

Jr. Bea: Is something wrong?

Gordon: Oh no, nothing at all. I just can't get used to the ringing in my ears. It hasn't stopped since I left the trenches.

Jr. Bea: What is it like to be in the front lines, day in and day out?

Gordon: For twenty hours a day, the earth shakes. It is quiet only when the guns are cooling. That usually happens for two hours shortly after darkness falls and again before dawn breaks. The first period of cessation is necessary because of the increased intensity of the guns to make the most of the declining day; the second to prepare for a vigorous resumption when light comes again.

Jr. Bea: *Sympathetically.* I've heard that life under constant fire is terrible.

Gordon: It's rough, but it's not the worst thing to live through. The most terrible thing I've experienced happened a few months ago.

Jr. Bea: What was that?

Gordon: *Absently, as though reliving the experience.* It was late at night. I was making my rounds in the trenches, checking on the men and making sure they were on alert. The German guns were booming and the star shells kept lighting up the sky.

I came to an isolated part of the trench, where a sentry was supposed to be keeping watch. He'd fallen asleep. That's a flagrant crime—if I had reported him, he'd have been court-martialed and executed. I simply couldn't let him die like that. So I woke him up and covered him with my revolver. I made him climb up into the open and held him there until the Germans shot him. Now his people believe he died gloriously in action.

The problem is that I can't seem to forget him. The experience was as unnerving to me as if I had bayoneted a dozen Germans. Every night, he visits me in my dreams, his body twisting as the bullets cut through him.

Jr. Bea is silent, aghast. They freeze.

Scene 25: Wartime Worries

Sr. Bea: The censor allowed my story to get through—despite the fact that it described a war crime of sorts. That officer could have woken the sentry and given him a warning. Even if he'd turned him in, his sentence might have been commuted. He reminded me of the generals who were running the war at the time—men who couldn't think beyond their rule books and didn't hesitate to sacrifice men's lives needlessly. They called it "necessary wastage," as though they were taking out the trash, rather than sending masses of men to certain death.

People on the home front were more preoccupied with their own survival than with what their men were facing. There were food shortages. Everything was rationed. You were allowed four pounds of bread and three ounces of meat per day, if you could get them. People stood in line for hours for each item of food. Sometimes a queue would form for butter. When the supply of butter ran out, they were told, "You may stay in this queue for bacon!" Slowly the line would move up for bacon until it was all gone. Then they would be told, "You may stay in this queue for cheese!" After everything was gone, a sign was posted: "No butter, no margarine, no bacon, no tea, no sugar," and on and on. Since I could only shop after work, there was often nothing left to buy. Like most women, I only ate one or two meals a day.

I knew I had become obsessed with food when I got caught in a subway train fire. There I was, between stations, the smoke billowing into my car. Yet all I could think about was how dreadful it was to die the very week that margarine was going to be available. Fortunately, a young female conductor came and guided us out of the train. It was after that episode that Guy Furniss came into my life again.

Scene 26: Guy Furniss Returns

Jr. Bea is in her office, reading over some papers. She looks tired and worn. An officer knocks and puts his head around the door. It is Guy Furniss. He is in uniform with a Scottish Glengarry cap.

Jr. Bea: *Flushed, excited.* Guy! I can't believe it's you. How have you been?

Guy: *Takes off his cap, smiles.* As well as you might think, given the fact that we're at war. I've been sent back to London for a few weeks to train new recruits.

Guy Furniss in uniform.
MONICA NEWTON COLLECTION

Roberta MacAdams in a promotional photograph.

Jr. Bea:	I got your letters.
Guy:	I got yours, although I would have liked a few more.
Jr. Bea:	*Trying to be casual.* The war got in the way. *Pause, as though something just occurred to her.* Anyway, I thought you were seeing Sibyl. Have you looked her up yet?
Guy:	I'd rather spend time with *you.* How about coming out to dinner with me tonight? If you can still tolerate me by the end of the meal, we'll follow it up with an evening at the theatre.
Jr. Bea:	*She is happy, excited, begins to stand.* Of course I'd be able to "tolerate" dinner with you. It would be . . . oh my . . . *she teeters, then faints.*
Guy:	Bea! *He drops down and gathers her in his arms.*

Scene 27: From Love To Politics

Sr. Bea:	*Smiling.* That fool carried me down three flights of stairs before he realized there was an elevator. Outside, he hailed a cab. The driver was low on gas and refused to take me to hospital. Guy pulled out his revolver and told the cabbie that he would be the next casualty of war if he didn't change his mind. He drove us to the hospital at breakneck speed. It turned out that I was only suffering from malnutrition. For the next few weeks Guy made sure that I ate more than I'd eaten since the war began. Where he found the food, I'll never know. After he went back to France, we wrote to each other every week.
Gladys:	Wasn't it around that time that you got involved in politics?
Sr. Bea:	In the spring of 1917, the Alberta government called a provincial election. The province's soldiers and

nurses were going to have two representatives. To be worthy of the name of suffragette I decided to ensure that at least one woman entered the race. I went from hospital to hospital, trying to get a nurse to stand for election. After being turned down several times, I remembered an Alberta girl working in a military hospital. She'd visited my office a few months before. Her name was Roberta MacAdams.

Scene 28: Finding A Candidate

Two chairs are set on each side of the tea trolley. It is set with a plate, a pot of tea, two cups, and two saucers. Nursing Sister Roberta MacAdams is pouring the tea, standing. She wears a white head scarf, indicating that she is a nursing sister. Jr. Bea is sitting in one of the chairs.

Roberta: *Formally.* Miss Nasmyth, I'm sorry I can't help you. I didn't enlist so that I could run for office. I've never been interested in voting or women's rights, for that matter. What good have they done women, anyway? Besides, I don't have the desire, time, or money to launch an election campaign! *She hands Jr. Bea a cup of tea.*

Jr. Bea: It's not about you and your needs or even what you believe about women's rights. It's about the men in the trenches. Don't you have a duty to the soldiers?

Roberta: Of course. There are a thousand beds in this hospital and every worker is needed. Staying here and doing my job is far more important than running for office.

Jr. Bea: You know very well that the broken men in this hospital have little to look forward to when they return home. Many will have to be retrained; some will never work again. Their families will carry impossible burdens. Why not fight for soldier's pensions and rehabilitation?

SOLDIERS AND NURSES FROM ALBERTA!!

You will have TWO VOTES at the forthcoming
Election under the Alberta Military Representation Act.

GIVE ONE VOTE TO THE MAN OF YOUR CHOICE AND
THE OTHER TO THE SISTER.

LOOK	LOOK
FOR	FOR
No. 14	No. 14
ON YOUR	ON YOUR
BALLOT PAPER!	BALLOT PAPER!

Miss ROBERTA CATHERINE MacADAMS,
Lieut. C.A.M.C., Ontario Military Hospital,
Orpington, Kent.

SHE WILL WORK NOT ONLY FOR YOUR BEST INTERESTS BUT FOR THOSE
OF YOUR WIVES, MOTHERS, SWEETHEARTS, SISTERS AND CHILDREN
AFTER THE WAR.

Remember those who have helped you so nobly through the fight.

Roberta MacAdams's campaign flyer.
MONICA NEWTON COLLECTION

Roberta:	I'm not sure anyone would listen to me . . .
Jr. Bea:	Why not? The soldiers know just how our nursing sisters have tried to give them every comfort.
Roberta:	I'm really a dietitian, not a nurse.
Jr. Bea:	But you have the same rank and the same uniform. The men will never know the difference. The main thing is that you are championing their rights.
Roberta:	Do you really believe this will enable me to do something good for the men?
Jr. Bea:	I do.
Roberta:	Then I accept your invitation. *The two women shake hands.*

Scene 29: Campaigning

Slide: campaign flyer.

Roberta MacAdams stands at centre stage, ready to give her campaign speech. Jr. Bea sits in a chair at one side of the stage.

Roberta:	I shall work for pensions for our soldiers, and I shall put my best efforts into plans for placing soldiers on the land when they return to Canada. Occupation must be found for our fighting forces and suitable training provided for them. After the war, there will be armies of men returning to Canada. Before 1914, these men built our railways, dug our ditches, built our bridges, and opened up our mining camps. When war came, they enlisted in the hundreds and thousands and they fought bravely and sacrificially. When the war is over one day—and that day will come sooner than later—they will return to Canada. After their experience, they will be a great, constructive army of peace. They must return to a country that is ready to help them rebuild their lives.

Jr. Bea: August 16, 1917. Dear Dad. Today is voting day—all ballots must be in by six o'clock. My candidate, Miss MacAdams, is glad the campaign is over. It's hard to believe that just a few weeks ago, we were demanding the support of Lord Beaverbrook, the owner of the *Daily Express*. He not only supported Miss MacAdams's candidacy, he promised to promote her campaign in his newspapers. After that, we had a photograph taken of Miss MacAdams. We put the picture on our campaign circular and had seven thousand printed for the men in England and France. Miss MacAdams took two weeks' leave. She wrote hundreds of letters to officers and nurses, and visited hospitals and military camps. Of course, we made enemies of the other candidates who are jealous of the attention she has received.

If all goes well, we will have made history. If she loses, all the fun we've had will have made it worthwhile. Furthermore, as publicity secretary for Alberta, the advertising to the province has more than justified all the time I've taken away from the office. Cross your fingers. I'll write again soon and let you know the results. Lots of love as always, Bea.

A British reporter enters and sits at the other side of the stage. He is on the phone.

Reporter: Take this down. I want it in tomorrow's issue of the *Times*. "Canadian nursing sister Roberta MacAdams M-A-C-capital-A-D-A-M-S has become the first woman elected to Parliament while on British soil. Miss MacAdams will serve in the Alberta legislature . . ." Alberta. A-L-B-E-R-T-A, like the prince. Now, as I was saying, "In that province, women share the burdens and responsibilities of citizenship. To those who have watched the slow progress of the women's cause in Britain, this straightforward and very matter-of-fact recognition of women's citizenship is refreshing. In comparison to Canadian women, the bitter struggle that the women of Britain continue to wage is a tragic waste of energy." Got that? Good—I've got to get going. I'm hoping the new lady MLA will give me a personal interview—

Scene 29: Victory

Sr. Bea: Roberta won her seat with over four thousand votes, seven hundred more than her nearest rival. I didn't have long to celebrate. I was too busy planning my trip to France.

Gladys: *Eager, interested.* I've heard about that tour. You and three others were the first Canadian women journalists officially allowed to tour the lines in France.

Sr. Bea: Roberta came with us—she wanted to visit her constituents before she returned to Alberta. Support for the war was flagging and military authorities thought that allowing a group of women journalists to tour the front might help with their propaganda efforts.

Gladys: Didn't you feel constrained, having the military determine where you went and what you saw?

Sr. Bea: No . . . Up until that point, just one member of our party had been given access to the front and only because she was living in France. Even the few male journalists who were allowed in the war zone had to become British officers. We accepted the restrictions in the knowledge that we would convey the truth to our readers as best we could. So many women back home depended on us to tell them what was *really* happening to their sons and daughters overseas.

Gladys: Daughters?

Sr. Bea: The nurses, WAACs, and ambulance drivers that were working in the line of fire . . .

Heather D. Swain as ambulance driver Grace MacPherson.
KAREN SIMONSON

Scene 30: Firing Lines

Slide: ambulance drivers and their ambulances. Jr. Bea and Grace MacPherson walk onto the stage. Both are wearing heavy winter coats. Grace is tough, boyish. She mimes polishing an ambulance and changing its tire as she speaks with Jr. Bea.

Jr. Bea: Grace, thank you so much for showing me around the hospital. It seems huge. How many patients are here?

Grace: About thirty thousand. It's not just one hospital, you know. There are twenty—two Canadian hospitals and another eighteen American, Australian, and British hospitals, as well as specialty hospitals.

Jr. Bea: What's that hospital there? *She points offstage.*

Grace: *Looking in the direction to which Jr. Bea is pointing.* Well, that's one we don't talk much about . . .

Jr. Bea: Why?

Grace: That's where they treat venereal disease. *Wicked smile.* Canadians make up the highest percentage of cases.

Jr. Bea: Somehow I'm not surprised. Tell me about your work as an ambulance driver. I understand that there are a large number of Canadian women driving ambulances to the front.

Grace: *Grace starts to work on changing her ambulance's tire.* Eleven months ago, the male ambulance drivers were replaced by women. There are a hundred of us. We look after sixty-five ambulances. When there is a big push, we work twenty-four hours a day. We unload ambulance trains and pick up men from clearing stations closer to the front. In a two-week period we have moved as many as twelve thousand men.

Jr. Bea: Have you ever come under fire?

Grace:	Oh, often. Sometimes when we are sent to pick up patients, a bombing raid begins. If it's too dangerous to keep driving, we sleep by the side of the road.
Jr. Bea:	It must be frightening . . .
Grace:	I don't mind. This is the job I came to do and I'm doing it. The biggest challenge is keeping our ambulances up to the job. They don't have windshields or lights. And their tires seem to get an awful lot of punctures. When that happens, we have to look after them, even if we're under fire.
Jr. Bea:	How do the soldiers react to a woman ambulance driver?
Grace:	They're all right. I don't give them a lot of sympathy, otherwise they'd break down, and I'd lose my sanity. I'll always remember the wounded from Vimy. There was one man who was moaning in the back of my ambulance. I told him "Cut that out! Nobody's riding in my ambulance moaning like that." "I got my leg off," he told me. I swallowed a bit and said, "Look, I bashed my thumb. Now you're going to get the best ride you ever had in your life." If I'd cried all over him, he might have lost his courage and wouldn't have survived the trip.
Jr. Bea:	What gives you the strength to do this work? You're only nineteen.
Grace:	*Firmly.* My brother died in the Dardanelles. I don't want his loss to be for nothing. So I'll just keep going until the end of the war or the end of me.

SX: a siren sounds. Sounds of bombing.

Lighting: searchlights criss-cross the stage.

| Grace: | I've got to go! |

She shakes hands with Bea and rushes off stage.

Scene 31: Air Raid

Slide: wrecked hospital at Étaples, France.

Jr. Bea: *Steps forward to the front of the stage to address the audience.* On a warm May evening, five months after our visit, fifteen German planes attacked the hospital at Étaples. In just two hours, they dropped one hundred and sixteen bombs. At one of the Canadian hospitals, a bomb made a direct hit on the nurses' quarters, setting them on fire. As stretcher bearers tried to pull survivors to safety, German planes flew low, spraying machine gun fire among the rescuers. Grace MacPherson was one of the stretcher bearers. Throughout the raid, she tended the wounded and transported them to less damaged hospitals. By the next morning, sixty people were dead or dying and another seventy-three were wounded.

Scene 32: Relevant Again

Sr. Bea: It's hard to believe that Canadians are going to be facing those bombs again. I've heard some people say that the war will be over by Christmas, just like they did back in 1914. But anyone who has lived through the first war knows that's a faint hope.

Gladys: I think you're right. It's going to take more than blind optimism to stop Hitler.

Sr. Bea: That's why it's good that you will be going overseas. You'll let people know what is really happening.

Gladys: Just like you did. I have a feeling that I'll face a lot of the same challenges that you did.

Sr. Bea: Does that mean you think I'm "relevant," after all?

Gladys: I'm sorry I said that. I have a feeling that your war and my war will be a lot alike.

Sr. Bea:	There will be some differences, I'm sure. But the basic reality won't change, men killing men, women mopping up, and reporters trying to tell their stories as truthfully as they can.
Gladys:	Can you tell us, what did you do during the last months of your war?
Sr. Bea:	Believe it or not, I fell in love again.

Scene 33: A Marriage Is Announced

Slide: bed-sitting room. Guy stands at one end of the stage, packing his suitcase. Now and again, he looks over at Bea. She is reading a letter to her parents.

Jr. Bea:	Dear Mother and Dad. The miles between us make it necessary for me to tell you the following news through the inadequate medium of a letter. "A marriage has taken place between Beatrice Nasmyth, daughter of Mr. and Mrs. James Nasmyth, and Captain Guy MacKenzie Furniss, son of Mr. and Mrs. Harry Furniss." I hope you will meet your new son-in-law soon. *She glances at Guy.* Until then, I can only describe him as someone with an immense sense of humour, a love of books and art, and the good taste to find my companionship absorbing—not having had much of it.
	I realize the cruelty of giving you such tremendous news all at once. Up until a few months ago, I had no intention of marrying Guy. Yet his bombardment was fierce and my reserves too few, so I finally accepted his proposal. Our entire acquaintance has been made up of brief meetings and speedy partings and centred round railway stations, hotels, and restaurants.

Guy walks over to Beatrice and puts his arms around her as she continues to read.

Guy arrived from France last month to the regimental depot where he has been improving the shining hours by lecturing. He is an expert in musketry and . . .

She struggles to remember.

Jr. Bea & Guy: *In unison, looking into each other's eyes.* Lewis guns.

Jr. Bea: However, Guy was under orders to proceed again to France, so we decided to act while we could.

Jr. Bea & Guy: *In unison.* These days, we can't plan ahead, we can only enjoy the present.

Guy walks back to his suitcase, shuts it, puts on his cap, and with an anguished look at Jr. Bea, carries the suitcase offstage.

Jr. Bea: *She watches him leave, then gathers her courage to end her letter.* I leave you to digest all of this. Remember, I'm almost as dazed as you are. Please write Guy a cheerful letter welcoming him into the family. A big wrench is coming. It makes my heart nearly stop beating to think of all the chances there are against your ever meeting him. All my love, Beatrice.

Scene 34: One Of The Lucky Ones

Sr. Bea: We had a three-day honeymoon before Guy left for France. *Pause.* In the end, I was one of the lucky ones. Guy survived. In 1919, we went to France again—I was assigned to cover the Versailles Peace Conference. It was my last job as a foreign correspondent. I was sick of war. I never wanted to see anyone in my family in khaki again. We moved home to Vancouver. I'm sure you won't be surprised to learn that I started writing fiction—love stories and poetry for *Maclean's* and *Chatelaine*.

Gladys: Did you have children?

Jenny McKillop as Beatrice Nasmyth and Randy Brososky as Guy Furniss.
KAREN SIMONSON

Sr. Bea: Oh yes. We had a daughter named Monica and a son named Harry. Monica became a teacher. As for Harry—a few years ago we sent him to a boy's boarding school. While he was away, he took flying lessons and got his pilot's license. Last month, he enlisted in the—

Gladys: RCAF.

Sr. Bea: I said goodbye to him this morning. They're shipping him overseas. So you see, your next big story will be mine, too.

The women gaze at one another as Second World War music builds and builds—could be "Tipperary," which was used in both wars, or some other Second World War tune, such as the chorus from "I'll Be Seeing You" or "We'll Meet Again."

End

John and Florence Brownlee, leaving the Edmonton
Law Courts building during the trial, June 1934.

RESPECTING THE ACTION FOR SEDUCTION

THE BROWNLEE AFFAIR

BY DAVID CHEOROS AND KAREN SIMONSON

Official portrait of John Brownlee, from during his time as premier.

JOHN EDWARD BROWNLEE

Alberta would not be what it is today were it not for the premiership of John E. Brownlee. He is responsible for the Natural Resources Transfer Agreement in 1929, something dreamed about since the establishment of the province in 1905, but not realized until much later, thanks to the leadership of John Brownlee. Brownlee's legacy has largely been overshadowed by the scandal that ended his time as premier and resulted in the downfall of the United Farmers of Alberta government in the 1935 general election.

Born August 27, 1883, in Norfolk County, Ontario, John Edward Brownlee was the son of William James and Christina (Shaw) Brownlee. Brownlee attended public school and later the Sarnia Collegiate Institute. He trained as a teacher and taught school in Bradshaw, Ontario, from 1902 to 1904. He then attended Victoria College (University of Toronto) and graduated with a bachelor of arts degree in 1908.

In 1909, Brownlee articled with the Calgary law firm of Lougheed, Bennett, Allison, and McLaws. He was admitted to the Alberta bar in 1912. On December 23, 1912, he married Florence Agnes Edy. They had two children: John Edy and Alan Marshall.

In 1913, he became a junior partner in the firm Muir, Jephson, and Adams. During his early years of practice, he did a considerable amount of legal work for the Alberta Farmers' Co-operative Elevator Company Limited (later known as the United Grain Growers Company). By 1917, Brownlee became general counsel for the United Grain Growers and was legal counsel to the United Farmers of Alberta. He also played a prominent part in the organization of the Alberta Wheat Pool.

Following the 1921 election, Brownlee became the Attorney General, even though he had not run in the election (he ran in a by-election later that year). Brownlee was appointed premier of Alberta on November 23, 1925, after the resignation of Premier Herbert Greenfield. The United Farmers accomplished a lot while in office, but they lead Alberta through the first years of the Depression— a difficult time throughout the province and continent.

In 1934, Brownlee was embroiled in a sex scandal, with major consequences to his political career. Those involved with the scandal gave widely disparate accounts of the facts. Following the suit brought against him by Vivian MacMillan, Brownlee resigned as premier, effective July 10, 1934. He continued to serve as MLA until he was defeated in the 1935 general election.

After leaving politics, Brownlee practised law in Edmonton, and was soon legal counsel for the United Grain Growers. In 1948, he was appointed president and general manager of the United Grain Growers, and moved to Calgary. Brownlee died on July 15, 1961, in Calgary.

In *Respecting the Action for Seduction*, Brownlee is fifty-three and the in-house counsel for the powerful United Grain Growers.

VIVIAN MACMILLAN

Vivian Almeda MacMillan was born June 10, 1912, in Nelson, British Columbia. She was the daughter of Allan Duncan and Letha MacMillan; Vivian's brother Harry was four years older than her. In 1920, the MacMillan family moved to Edson, Alberta, where Vivian's father was employed as assistant foreman in the Canadian National Railway shop. Vivian attended Edson Public School and High School, and the family regularly attended Edson's Baptist Church, where Vivian played organ and taught Sunday school.

In 1929, Vivian began her Grade 11 year at school, which was the highest grade at Edson High School at the time. This was the same year that Carl Snell began teaching Latin at the school; Vivian was one of his students. As a Baptist churchgoer, Carl became a family friend of the MacMillans and often attended Sunday dinner at their

Vivian MacMillan, the "Girl in the Red Studebaker."

home. Carl proposed to Vivian in the spring of 1930, but she refused on the grounds she was too young. As she could not continue to Grade 12 in Edson, Vivian contemplated further studies in music or nursing elsewhere, though her father wanted her to remain in Edson and continue her music studies there.

Vivian met John Brownlee when he was campaigning in Edson in 1930. She was seventeen at the time. Brownlee encouraged her to come to Edmonton and study business. In August 1930, Vivian moved to Edmonton to take a business course at Alberta College. She finished these studies in June 1931. She started working in the office of the Attorney General in July. In the fall of 1932, she met a young medical student, John Caldwell, the son of Reverend J. Caldwell. John proposed to her in January of 1933. That same year, Vivian and her father formally accused Brownlee of seduction. This was essentially the procurement of sex through misrepresentation, a criminal offense at that time.

Following the trial in June of 1934, Vivian returned to her life in Edson. On August 7, 1935, she married Henry Sorenson, of Edson, who operated an ice cream parlour there. They had one son, Allan Crestin, born about 1938. Vivian moved to Calgary in 1940, likely around the time Henry enlisted to fight in the Second World War. Upon his return, Vivian and Henry divorced, and Vivian became the bookkeeper for a construction company operated by Frank Howie. By March of 1949, Frank and Vivian were having an affair and Frank divorced his wife in 1950. Vivian and Frank were married shortly afterward. Their son, Michael, was born in 1955. Vivian and Frank later moved to the Okanagan, then to Arizona, and finally to Florida. Vivian died August 1, 1980, in Florida.

In *Respecting the Action for Seduction*, Vivian is twenty-five and working in her husband's ice cream parlour in Edson, Alberta.

Kirsten Rasmussen as Vivian MacMillan and Steve Pirot as John Brownlee, photographed in front of the Alberta Legislature. Promotional photo for the first production, 2008.
IAN JACKSON/EPIC PHOTOGRAPHY

Respecting the Action for Seduction premiered at the Roxy Theatre, Edmonton, Alberta, on July 28, 2008, with the following company:

John Brownlee	Steve Pirot
Florence Brownlee	Steve Pirot
Neil Maclean	Steve Pirot
A.L. Smith	Steve Pirot
Vivian MacMillan	Kirsten Rasmussen
Florence Brownlee	Kirsten Rasmussen
Director	David Cheoros
Costume Designer	Geri Dittrich
Lighting Designer	Paul Bezaire

The production ran approximately sixty minutes.

SET

A small room in an Ottawa court building on March 1, 1937. In the original production, there were two chairs and a coat rack. All court scenes are taken verbatim from transcripts.

COSTUMES

Costumes reflect the 1920s. John Brownlee wears a pinstripe suit with a white high-collared shirt and tie. Vivian Sorenson wears a simple calf-length skirt and matching blouse.

CHARACTERS

Over the course of the play, the characters of John and Vivian step into various roles: younger versions of themselves, caricatures of themselves, and other characters such as Florence Brownlee, Neil Maclean, and A.L. Smith. In the original production, it was intended that it always be John and Viv themselves stepping into these roles. However, it may be equally useful to have the two actors move entirely into the smaller roles, or to assign these roles to other actors in an expanded cast.

Scene 1

John enters, settles. Vivian enters, sees John, and starts to exit.

John: It's no longer improper that we speak. We won't be called on to testify any more.

Viv: Thank God. *She starts to enter.*

John: Although I'd prefer that you leave the door open. I don't want to be accused of assaulting you. Again.

Viv: Funny. *She makes herself comfortable.* How are you, John?

John: Well enough.

Viv: You look tired.

John: The United Grain Growers are keeping me busy. How are you, Miss MacMillan?

Viv: Not "Miss" anymore.

John: Ah. Congratulations. The promising medical student.

Viv: Johnny Caldwell? God, no. Promising medical student! He promised me a happy life together. He promised me a way out. He is very well settled into practice. No. After the trial, I retreated to Edson and Henry. Henry runs an ice cream parlour. He's sweet.

John: Well, I'm happy for you.

Viv: And Florence is well?

Scene 2

John becomes Florence. The Brownlee home, spring 1933.

John: Come in, Vivian, dear! We're just setting for supper. It's been far too long since we last saw you. You've been awfully busy.

A quick but warm embrace.

John: Perhaps with that young Johnny Caldwell?

Viv: He's so wrapped up in his examinations; I think I've entirely left his head. The peaches down at Riley's looked fresh and heavenly, so I bought a basket for our dessert.

John: Such a peach *you* are, dear. This early in the season, they must have cost you a fortune. Well, we'll have to save Mr. Brownlee's for later—he's out at a constituency meeting, but should be back in time to drive you home.

Viv: I'm sure he will.

John: Pardon, dear?

Viv: I'm sure you're right. Would we have a few minutes to sit before supper?

John: Of course. I am so happy with the garden this year. Although just when I thought I'd seen the last of the aphids on my roses, I've started to see blackness on the buds again. Can you believe how persistent those vermin can be?

Viv: Mm-hm.

John: Listen to me. You wanted to talk about something. Is it work? You mentioned that Mr. Smailes is sometimes a bit short with you. We'll have to get Mr. Brownlee to say something. Oh! Everything's falling into place for the trip to Pincher Creek next month. The boys are so looking forward to the change of scenery. We have a wager on how many work files Mr. Brownlee will sneak into the trunks.

Viv: I'm so glad you're all getting away. John's seemed so drawn of late.

John: Ah, Vivian. It might be considered proper in the rural areas for you to refer to your elders by their first names. But in the city and especially in the legislature it is proper only for you to refer to him as Mr. Brownlee or Premier Brownlee.

Viv: Of course. Thank you. I'm going to go see if there's something I can do to help Jean with dinner.

John: Yes. And you're welcome to spend as much time as you wish here while we're gone. Jean will be away visiting family, so it'll be catch as catch can for meals, but surely it would be more comfortable than that rooming house.

Viv: Thanks ever so much, Mrs. Brownlee. I can lie in John's bed and dream of him.

John: What was that, dear?

Rewind.

Viv: Thanks ever so much, Mrs. Brownlee, but I can't bear the guilt of this affair any longer, and I'm going to break it off tonight.

John: What was that, dear?

Rewind.

Viv: Thanks ever so much, Mrs. Brownlee.

John: Some tea before supper, Vivian?

Both actors make the same motions as Florence. John becomes himself in 1934 and Vivian becomes Florence.

Viv: Some tea before supper, John? We've run out of cream, but I could add milk. It's not so very late. Jean might have time to—

John: Florence, it's fine. You fuss overmuch sometimes.

Viv: Well, sometimes you need fussing over. All your work, the political meetings, the federal banking commission. And now this.

John: Her testimony is almost finished. A few supporting witnesses, and soon we'll be able to tell the true story. This will all vanish in the cold, clean, light of day.

Viv: *Refers to paper.* "Pictured the premier as a love torn, sex-crazed victim of passion and jealousy. That she owed it as a sacred duty to the wife of the premier to submit lest he throw up the reins of office or send his wife to death as the victim of childbed agonies."

John: Don't worry, dear. Smith will demolish this. It may not even be necessary for you to provide corroborating testimony.

Viv: Testimony? What could I possibly say? That I took this viper into our home, drank tea, and supped with her a hundred times? That I have the judgment in character of an imbecile?

John: Hush, no. You might need to confirm our sleeping arrangements. And also that our relations are perfectly normal and healthy.

Viv: Of course, John. I will be prepared.

John: I love you, Florence.

Viv: Yes.

Back to 1937.

John: Florence is just fine. Why are we here, Miss . . . Mrs. . . .

Viv: Sorenson.

John: The Court of Appeal's decision in my favour should have ended this foolishness.

Viv: The jury—

John: —was overruled by Justice Ives, and you were ordered to pay costs.

Viv: That fossil. He had no right—

John: So your lawyer said, with some vehemence, at the Supreme Court of Alberta. I do hope you're paying Neil Maclean well.

Viv: He's not taking a dime—says he just wants to get the bastards.

John: Well, if your intent—sorry, if Maclean's intent—was to bring down the government, you did a whizz-bang job. The Social Credit crackpots are about to celebrate their second anniversary in office and Maclean's liberals were left out in the cold.

Viv: And without you at the helm, the United Farmers just blew away? How arrogant.

John: Meanwhile, here we are. The Supreme Court of Canada. Your father must be feeling the pinch.

Viv: A second mortgage. He's managing. My uncles have pitched in.

John: I can't imagine that even ten thousand dollars would have made this all worth it.

Viv: Don't even pretend it's about the money. What happened to that man who danced me five times around the hall in Edson?

John: Ah yes. Our first meeting. How did you and Maclean describe it in court?

Scene 3

Vivian becomes twenty-two, starting testimony. John becomes Maclean, her attorney.

John: You had been introduced at a reception, I believe, when he was in Edson with the Honourable Henry Pattinson for a fundraising event?

Viv: Yes, Mr. Maclean. When the party came to get into our car, there was some discussion as to where would be the most comfortable place for Mother to ride. Mr. Brownlee suggested she ride in the front with her husband, and Premier Brownlee would ride in the back seat with Mr. Pattinson's son and myself.

John: Mr. Brownlee?

Viv: On the right hand side.

John: Pattinson's boy?

Viv: In the centre.

John: And you were on the left in the back?

Vivian becomes a teenager. John becomes a suave, animated, younger version of himself. Standing side by side, squeezed in a couple of feet apart.

John: Nonsense. Your parents are a very important part of this community, and it's a pleasure to be here. In Edson.

Viv: Well, it's certainly an honour to have you here, Premier Brownlee.

John: John. *Calling into the front seat.* You have a beautiful daughter here, Mrs. MacMillan. Mayor. What are you going to do with her? Will she stay home or come in to Edmonton and complete her education?

Viv: Well, I don't even know yet if I've passed my Grade 11 examinations. But I've awfully enjoyed playing the organ at church. I thought perhaps I'd go down to Mount Royal College to study music and the humanities.

John: Hmm. A useless occupation, music. Very little money in it, I believe, and it seems to take a great while to get anywhere at all.

Viv: Well, I had thought to take up nursing. Mother says it's a noble profession, and then I could go and study at the Royal Alex Hospital. Father objects, though. Says that it's too hard a life for a girl.

John: Well . . . I'm sure it is very hard. Not so very challenging for a girl like you, is it?

Viv: Sorry?

John: Nursing. Have you considered business? Stenography, administration—the gears of commerce. It's an excellent time to be in business, Vivian.

Viv: Business? I'm not certain that I would care for that kind of work.

John: Come, miss. You are travelled, you are well spoken, and you seem quite reasonable. Already, you outpace by two points most of the opposition.

Viv: But even then, I'm not sure what kind of job I could get afterward. There are a lot of girls looking for office jobs now.

John: I'm sure that something could be arranged for you.

Viv: Well, regardless, my parents have rather decided that I should stay home another year, because I am too young to leave home.

John: Friends, I can assure you. If she comes to Edmonton, she should be very welcome in my home. She won't be alone in a strange city.

Viv: What do you say? Mother?

Scene 4

John breaks away to 1937.

John: To suggest that I would have made such a commitment on the spur of the moment. That I . . . "Took an immediate shine to you."

Viv: We danced five times at the dinner. All night, I felt your eyes on me. And you still deny that you were on the telephone with me a week after I arrived in Edmonton? "This is Mr. Brownlee speaking. A little birdie told me you were in town. I would like to have you come over to my home Sunday afternoon, and meet Mrs. Brownlee and the boys."

Dear sainted Florence. Amazing she stood by you through everything.

John: I gave her no reason to do otherwise.

Viv: Driving me home a few weeks later, a Sunday night, offering to show me the new public works projects.

John: Still! Even with just the two of us here. You're still—

Viv: Stopping on that country road. The night warm for October.

She settles into the massive Studebaker. He follows reluctantly.

John: I hope you're liking Edmonton.

Viv: It's nice. Big. It took a while to get used to the smell.

John: Ah yes. It'll improve now—we've just passed Bill 56, the coal mines in town will be shutting down soon. But listen to me—all business. I've certainly enjoyed your visits to our home. You're a real ray of sunshine.

Viv: That's kind of you, Premier Brownlee.

John: John. You are a very beautiful girl, Vivian. Do you mind if I ask you—

Viv: Ask me?

John: Ask you what you know. About life.

Viv: Well, I don't know exactly what you mean, but I suspect that I probably know as much as any other girl of eighteen does.

John: I expect you do.

Viv: Sir?

John: Vivian, I think you should come out with me more often. Edmonton's a big, bustling place. Full of opportunity. I could be a very good guardian and guide for you. And I could certainly appreciate your help as well, Vivian. It's a very lonely time, a very hard time for me right now. The pressures of office are proving to be quite extraordinary. I could certainly use a pal. Someone entirely apart from my problems. You have been to my home several times.

Viv: It's a beautiful—

John: Yes, yes. I share a room with my son Jack. Florence shares with our younger, Alan.

Viv: I . . . yes?

John: Vivian, Florence and I have not been . . . as man and wife for years. After Alan was born, she was quite ill. She told you about her visit to the Mayo Brothers clinic? The doctors thought it would be dangerous for her to conceive again. So, you see, it's a dangerous thing. I'm very concerned for Florence's health. And I feel that you could help with that. The pressure, it's building in me. It's beginning to seriously affect my ability to concentrate at work. And I can't bear to think of endangering Florence.

Viv: She is a most genteel woman. And she's been very kind to me.

John: Well, I can think of a way that you could show your gratitude to Mrs. Brownlee, and to myself.

Viv: Perhaps there's some other way.

John: This. This is the only way.

Viv: Please no!

He lunges at her. She fends him off. He resumes his 1937 demeanour.

John: Preposterous!

She responds by stepping back into courtroom mode.

Viv: The next week, on the ride home, Premier Brownlee told me that he had been madly in love with me from the start, and that surely I must have known it. I told him I had not been aware. And then Mr. Brownlee said—

John: "It is rather crowded in the front, is it not?"

Vivian MacMillan is escorted into the Edmonton
Law Courts by her attorney, Neil MacLean.

Viv: So we got into the back seat. He was kissing me, and had his arms around me. And I fought against him but on this occasion he gained partial entrance. Because I resisted so much he flew into a rage and got back in the front and drove back into Edmonton and down to the government garage.

John: *As Maclean.* You said he gained partial entrance. It is very distasteful, I know, but would you mind telling me just exactly what he did do?

Viv: When he forced me down on to the back seat of the Studebaker, he still had one arm around me to hold me in place, and with his other hand he raised my clothing, unfastened his own clothing, and then he tried to have sexual intercourse with me.

They shift back into 1937.

John: There was no assault. I drove you home that night.

Viv: Yes. But your lawyer—Smith—"The finest cross examiner in the province"—

John: Don't believe everything you read in the papers.

Viv: —tried to dispute it on logistical grounds!

Vivian returns to court. John becomes A.L. Smith, Brownlee's defense lawyer.

John: So getting into the back seat that night, you still had no idea he wanted to have intercourse with you?

Viv: I did not think he could have intercourse with me in the back seat of a car.

John: I do not think so yet. You were lying flat, were you, parallel with the back seat?

Viv: Yes.

John: And you fought as hard as you could?

Viv: Yes.

John: Did you put a mark on him?

Viv: No, sir.

John: Eh?

Viv: Not that I know of.

John: So, we find him with one arm around your shoulder and the other raising your clothes and getting on top of you. You, a one-hundred-and-forty-pound girl, fighting your best in that back seat to save your honour. Is that the situation?

Viv: Yes, sir.

John: And on this particular night. When did you make up your mind that it was a proper thing for you to have intercourse with the man to repay his wife's kindness?

Viv: Not on that night, sir.

They step back into the situation of the car. A few weeks later.

John: So strange that I have to wait until I'm forty-six—virtually an old man—to finally meet the woman I love. I've been premier for six years. A few more projects and I can retire. Leave public life and the public eye. We could find a place somewhere. A villa in Italy. You're trembling. What's wrong?

Viv: I'm . . . I'm afraid of becoming pregnant.

John: Well, you needn't concern yourself. I took the liberty of consulting a physician. A very discreet, reputable man.

He pulls a small box of pills from his pocket and presses it into her hand.

Now, you just take one of those at the end of each month, just before you, you know. Then everything will be safe and fine for both of us.

Viv: Thank you.

He breaks away to 1937. She follows suit.

Scene 5

John: Large black pills in an unmarked box, conveniently lacking a name or a prescription! Perhaps a bit of fantasy contributed by your almost-fiancé the medical student. It's the least that he could do, really. For the five thousand he hoped to make in your little project.

Viv: Leave Johnny out of this.

John becomes Maclean again. Vivian takes the stand.

John: And who was John Caldwell?

Viv: Johnny is the son of the Reverend Caldwell and at that time he was taking medicine at the University of Alberta.

John: Were you fond of him?

Viv: We got along very well. I met him in the summer of 1932. He phoned me up and asked me if I would like to go out with him. I said I would. And we started going around together, and we soon found that we were quite in love with each other.

John: And did this have any effect on your relations with Mr. Brownlee?

Viv: It made me want more than ever to get away from him.

John: Would he consent?

Viv: He told me I knew what would happen if I broke off with him. That it would cost Mrs. Brownlee her life. I would be out of a job and he would certainly see that I did not get another position in the province of Alberta. But when I started seeing Johnny, I began to realize what a big mistake I had made.

They're back to 1937.

John: Johnny. Gold-digging little weasel. Following us around in a rental car.

Kirsten Rasmussen as Vivian MacMillan and Steve Pirot as John Brownlee, photographed
in front of the Alberta Legislature. Promotional photo for the first production, 2008.
IAN JACKSON/EPIC PHOTOGRAPHY

Viv: I swear, I knew nothing about that foolish car chase until after. It was just the one night, and I put a stop to that.

John: I should hope so. I was picturing that it was some irate voter out to change the electoral map.

Viv: I suppose, since Maclean was in the car too, that's not far from the truth. We didn't really talk politics until after the trial.

Scene 6

John becomes Maclean and Vivian is herself on the stand.

John: And when did you finish your business course at Alberta College?

Viv: June 1931.

John: Did you get a diploma or certificate?

Viv: No I did not.

John: There is no diploma for that course?

Viv: There is, but I had not got one.

John: So, without a diploma, what did you do, and what was done as far as you know, about getting a position in the spring or summer of 1931?

Viv: Mrs. Brownlee said she should think a government position could be very easily arranged. Then, a week before I left Alberta College, and Mr. Brownlee was out of the city, I thought: "Well. Perhaps I had better go down and see Mr. Smailes myself."

John: Who is Mr. Smailes?

Viv: He is the civil service commissioner. I thought while Mr. Brownlee was out of the city it would be a good time for me to go down to see about a position. I did not want him to think I was depending on him for getting a position. I went to see Mr. Smailes that afternoon and filled out an application. Mr. Smailes asked me to come into his office and he asked me if I was ready to go to work. I said yes. And I was sent to work in the Attorney General's department.

John: Where is that in relation to Mr. Brownlee's office?

Viv: It is on the same floor with Mr. Brownlee's office, on the same corridor.

John: Did you talk about this with Mr. Brownlee, after he came back?

Viv: When we were out one evening, he said, "I suppose you think you are rather clever, going down there and getting a position for yourself. It was all arranged for you."

John: How did it happen that you first slept at the Brownlee household?

Viv: It was the spring of 1932. Their maid, Jean, was going home for a month. It was seeding time on her farm. Mrs. Brownlee did not want to get a strange maid in the house for such a short time, and she thought that perhaps I would like to come over and stay with her, and we would just get along without a maid.

John: You had the maid's room?

Viv: Yes.

John: How far is it from the door of the maid's bedroom to Mr. Brownlee's door?

Viv: Five or six steps.

John: And the bathroom. Where is it?

Viv: It is at the head of the stairs.

And so, after everyone else was asleep, Mr. Brownlee would get up and come out into the hall and go down to the bathroom and run the water. That covered any noise I would make in getting out of bed in the maid's room.

On his way back, as he passed the maid's room, he would take hold of my hand and take me into his room and I would walk in his footsteps so it sounded only as if one person was walking. He would stand up between the two beds and I would get into his bed behind his back.

John: And why should he not have come into the maid's room?

Viv: The floor and the bed in the maid's room squeak.

John: And this happened on many occasions.

Viv: It happened nearly every night I was there.

Scene 7

John becomes Smith.

John: So in this city of eighty or ninety thousand people, and your parents in Edmonton occasionally and a long distance telephone you used frequently . . . here you were, having intercourse with this man from terror. Is that your story?

Viv: From terror, and because he told me it was my duty to do it. And he seemed to have an influence over me, which I could not break.

John: Influence you could not break? Did he hypnotize you?

Viv: No, Mr. Smith.

John: I want to turn to the incident at the house in the spring of 1932. On those occasions, Mr. Brownlee went into this room with the squeaky floors?

Viv: He did not come in. He just went past the door and down to the bathroom.

John: And sometimes he flushed the toilet and ran the taps?

Viv: Well, he always flushed the toilet and ran the taps.

John: He would get up out of bed and walk down to the bathroom, which was close to his wife's room?

Viv: Yes.

John: And how long would he let them run?

Viv: Well, the flushing of the toilet and the running of the taps was to cover any sound getting out the maid's bed. And walking across the squeaky floor and standing in the doorway.

John: Now. Do you know of any better way to disturb a household that has gone to sleep than to flush the toilet and run the taps at night? Do you know of any better way to wake them up? Do you? You have lived in lots of houses. Do you know of any way by which they could be more easily wakened than by flushing toilets and running taps close to them?

Viv: Well, I suppose it does wake people.

John: We will let that go. Then you say that you went into this room where his boy was sleeping?

Viv: Yes.

John: And took off the lower half of your pyjamas, you told me in discovery.

Viv: Yes.

John: And he took off the lower half of his?

Viv: Yes.

John: And he had connection with you?

Viv: Yes.

John: And his boy sleeping just eighteen inches away, the width of the bed stand table?

Viv: Yes.

John: And the light right at his hand on the bedside table between the two beds?

Viv: Yes.

John: And the boy never wakened?

Viv: No, only on one night.

John: Tell us about it.

Viv: Jack moved in bed and sort of mumbled to himself and Mr. Brownlee turned on the light to see if he was all right.

John: With you in bed with him?

Viv: With me in bed with him.

John: Well, courage is a marvellous thing.

Scene 8

Both: *As Smith, repeating a characteristic gesture.* Let me be clear about this.

Viv: *She becomes Smith, he Brownlee on the stand.* In 1930, when Vivian MacMillan came to Edmonton, you were premier, a lawyer and King's Counsel, and forty-six years of age?

John: That is correct.

Viv: And she was eighteen years of age, a country girl without previous city experience?

John: She was eighteen. She came from Edson. She was a girl, I think, who could take her place in any company. She was not a poor country girl, if you mean by that an inexperienced girl, and I use that in the best sense. I am not suggesting anything improper when I use that term.

Viv: What was the occasion of your going to Edson?

John: Mr. Pattinson, the MLA for that district, invited me to spend a day at Edson. It was an official visit.

Viv: Do you remember what you did in the morning?

John: The usual. Meeting some of the businessmen, visiting the schools, the hospital.

Viv: Mr. Brownlee. We have been told of a conversation with respect to the future of Miss MacMillan. You might tell me your recollection of that conversation.

His version of the back-of-car chat. He is awkward, she is fawning, star-struck.

John: Allan, Letha, it's so good to see you again, and to meet, ah . . .

Viv: Vivian. It's certainly an honour to meet you, Premier. And on my eighteenth birthday!

John: Er, yes, congratulations. And what are your plans for your further studies, miss?

Viv: Well, I've awfully enjoyed playing the organ at church. I thought perhaps I'd go down to the University of Alberta. Mother, though, would very much like me to take up nursing. She says that it is the noblest thing a girl can do.

John: Well . . . I'm sure it is, Miss MacMillan. Also very hard work, nursing. You may also wish to look at studies in business. The province is an oyster for a man. Er. Girl. With determination and a head for commerce.

Viv: Business? Oh, well, of course I'll look into it, Premier.

John: Well, if you do decide to study in Edmonton, perhaps Florence and I could have you to dinner some evening.

Viv: Oh, thank you! That's most, most kind, sir!

Scene 9

Viv: *She slips back to 1937.* That's not . . .

John: Once the shoe is on the other foot, it pinches.

Viv: *She takes on the role of Smith, as he takes the stand.* Miss MacMillan says you took her driving in the country on that

Monday night. Told her you were a very lonely man, that you needed a pal in order to permit you to carry on with your heavy duties. That your wife was an invalid and to have intercourse with her meant her life. That you thought it was Vivian MacMillan's duty to be as a wife to you to repay your wife's courtesies. Did you say those things to her?

John: I never said anything of that kind to Vivian MacMillan at any time.

Viv: She says that on that occasion you were driving in this big Studebaker car. Were you using that Studebaker car for the month of October?

John: I was not.

Viv: What car were you driving?

John: A Hupmobile 8, five passenger, which we purchased the sixth of September.

Viv: She then says that you telephoned her on Monday the twenty-seventh of October making arrangements to go out with her on Tuesday night the twenty-eighth. That you took her out and had intercourse with her that night. Did you?

John: I was not in the city on the Tuesday.

Viv: Where were you?

John: I drove to Stettler where I addressed the chamber of commerce at seven o'clock.

Viv: *She drops the character of Smith.* The trial was three years later. I was bound to get a few things wrong!

John: What was that, Mr. Smith?

Viv: *She resumes the character of Smith.* In all these times you drove Vivian MacMillan home, you have never kissed her?

John: No.

Viv: Have you ever had any desire to kiss her while you were out on those drives?

John: No.

Viv: Have you ever had any sexual desire for her whatever?

John: No.

Viv: She has said that she, a number of times, asked you for her freedom, and urged you to let her be free. To let her go. Did she ever do that?

John: Vivian MacMillan could have stopped coming to our house any time she chose.

Scene 10

Back to 1937.

Viv: Oh, poor, poor John. Reduced to being a mere corporate lawyer. I was still the "Girl in the Red Velvet Studebaker." Tourists stop by the ice cream parlour to take pictures. Depending on who you ask, I'm either a lying, conniving bitch, or else your whore.

John: I never said a word, a word against—

Viv: No, but there were plenty of hatchets in the party waiting to do it for you. Not to mention the private detectives you hired. Hiding a police stenographer under the bed and trying to trip Johnny up.

John: But to say all those things. To say that we had intercourse in Florence's bed.

Viv: You really don't understand.

John: Understand what?

Viv: I believed—

John: What?

Viv: You don't remember what happened. That first time you drove me home?

John: Which first time? The one you talked about, or the one I talked about?

Viv: It's just the two of us here.

John: This is a bad game, Vivian. Dangerous.

She mimes entering the car. John hesitates.

Viv: No stenographer under the bed here.

Scene 11

John begins driving the car. The first time he drove her home.

John: A beautiful night.

Viv: I can't thank you enough for having me over for dinner. After two weeks of the YWCA's watery mashed potatoes, it seemed like heaven.

John: I was surprised you didn't choose to stay in the new women's dormitory. It would have been more convenient for your studies.

Viv: Sure, but an eight o'clock curfew! I wouldn't be able to enjoy any sights of the big city. Concerts, lectures. Did you know that scientists have determined that it isn't just electrical nerve impulses from our brain that control our bodies? Our parts all talk to each other using special chemicals—"hormones"—that share instructions back and forth. And none of this is created by our thoughts. Imagine! All the ideas we have, all the things that we strive to accomplish—that's only a small part of the work our bodies are doing.

John: Like when my bladder is telling me when to go?

Viv: And not just your bladder. It's believed that some hormones are designed to leave the body and travel to other people, to send signals there.

John: Do you mean that strangers passing me on the street are sending me secret signals? Seems dreadfully complicated and random. Wouldn't a memo be more efficient?

Viv: I think that these messages are not so easily put into words.

John: Huh. I've spent the last decade trying to find succinct, clear arguments to steward this province, while what I really should have been doing is learning how to squirt out a more convincing set of chemicals.

Viv: Something like that. You must be doing something right, though. My father's no fan of the United Farmers, but he speaks very highly of you.

John: Tell him that I'll be pleased to count on his vote.

Viv: I wouldn't go that far. But he liked the way you got the crown land away from Ottawa. And the way you usually mean what you say.

John: Usually? *He splutters toward a response. She giggles. He smiles.*

Viv: If you don't mind me asking, you seemed a bit distracted at dinner this evening.

John: I don't want to burden you with affairs of state.

Viv: I will remind you that women have been voting on affairs of state for a long time.

John: A long time?

Viv: Since I was a little girl! Surely that's long enough for women to be treated with equality in your "affairs of state." *Mock severity.* Mr. Premier, I am a voting citizen of Alberta, and I demand a précis of the business of the province.

John: Demand? Very well, Miss MacMillan. It's this matter of the Turner Valley gas reserves. Now that we've actually pried control of the resources away from the federals, I've realized that my ministry had no plan for what to *do* with it. The oil producers in Turner Valley are just burning off the natural gas to get to the liquid naphtha because the naphtha's easier to transport.

Viv: I read about this in the *Bulletin*!

John: The province is losing nine million cubic feet of gas a day. So we've proposed a cap of one hundred million cubic feet per day.

Viv: To encourage them to actually use the gas.

John: Exactly. Since current production is more than five times that, you can imagine the squeal that's gone up among the investors. But I can't understand how a government could avoid thinking these resources need careful rationing.

Viv: Still, you need to recognize the investment of the oilmen.

John: Indeed.

Viv: Well, who benefits from the cap on the gas?

John: The pipeline would service Calgary—gives the residents a guaranteed and stable energy supply.

Viv: And they were some of the ones shouting for this cap, right?

John: Among the loudest.

Viv: Well, why not get them to help with the oil investors?

John: You mean, politically?

Viv: I mean money. A surtax on gas bills, going to producers to offset their costs. Everybody a little unhappy, but no one is outraged.

John: Fascinating. Possible. You just thought of this?

Viv: My father taught me the art of negotiation. After watching him work out a deal between a Bohunk farmer and a Frenchie trapper, nothing seems hard.

John: I shall have to watch out for my job with you around, Miss MacMillan.

Scene 12

Back to 1937.

Viv: I've never—No one else is as much fun to talk to, John.

John: Yes.

Viv: Even when you tormented me.

Four months after the first time he drove her home. Vivian in John's office. He is packing up files. She is bored.

John: Your classes are proceeding satisfactorily, Miss MacMillan?

Viv: I believe so, sir. Some of the teachers seem to have a great deal of experience. And some of the girls are just brilliant mates.

John: A calm and capable girl is an asset to any enterprise. I've often told Miss Brown that I would never have gotten re-elected without her keeping me on track. Clear thought, preparation, and, of course, excellent shorthand.

Viv: Shorthand?

John: How is your shorthand?

Viv: I'm working hard at it.

John: Indeed. Perhaps you need to work a good deal harder. Take this down.

Viv: What?

She scrambles to pick up a fountain pen and pad of paper. John initially dictates at a leisurely pace, and picks up gradually. She tries to keep up.

John: To the Right Honourable Richard Bedford Bennett. Re: your appointment of James Searles to oversee the Western Canadian Public Works Initiative. Paragraph.

It is with the greatest disappointment that I read of your selection. While Mr. Searles has some of the requisite experience, it seems that he has spent a grand total of six weeks in the Prairies, four of those on trains to or from the port of Vancouver. Paragraph.

I have no desire to cast aspersions on his alma mater, Dalhousie University. It is a good enough school for those who like such things. But we in Alberta set our sights a good deal higher . . .

She finally gives up and hurls the pad at him in frustration. He laughs, she glares, then joins him in laughing.

Viv: You, sir, have the laugh of a scoundrel.

John: And you, Vivian, the smile of an angel.

Eye contact. Something passes between them. Back to 1937.

Scene 13

Viv: Tell me I imagined that.

John: You flatter yourself. Or me. Just an old fool trying to help a pretty girl.

Viv: The help went both ways. You didn't mind when I gave you that massage.

John: Massage?

Viv: That time that you had an awful cold. I rubbed your back.

John: You never!

Viv: I recall quite distinctly. While the House was in session, a hammer blow to the head wouldn't get you out of the office before ten at night. Your cold must have been terrible.

John: Ah yes!

Viv: Mustard plaster, two layers of cheesecloth, and a good rub. And then the next day, you were back in the legislature. At Sunday dinner, you said that it was all thanks to your personal nurse.

John: I'm sorry to say, but . . . the plaster . . . well, it was actually quite . . .

Viv: What?

John: The next day, the speaker commented on my attentiveness. Truth be told, I couldn't lean back in my chair.

Viv: Oh Christ.

John: I think you put in too much mustard powder.

Viv: This is mortifying. I built it all up to be—

John: I didn't mean . . .

Viv: But I didn't do anything for you.

John: Well, not that time. But in conversations, your presence in our home.

Viv: Like a daughter.

John: Not entirely.

Viv: On the stand, you certainly came across in a fatherly way. "Miss MacMillan seemed to us a great, vivacious, decent-living girl."

John: If I had been your father, I'd have put a stop to your running around with Johnny Caldwell.

Viv: Even before the trial, it was pretty clear you disliked him.

John: I attribute most of my feelings about your engagement to his utter worthlessness. He pulled at his fingers when we spoke. What kind of a doctor tries to dislocate his own finger joints?

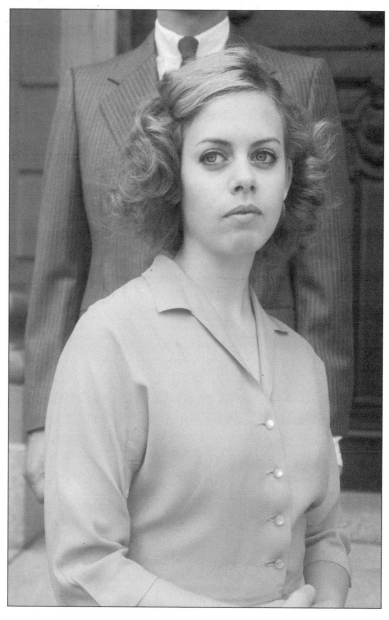

Kirsten Rasmussen as Vivian MacMillan and Steve Pirot as John Brownlee, photographed in front of the Alberta Legislature. Promotional photo for the first production, 2008.
IAN JACKSON/EPIC PHOTOGRAPHY

Viv: You interrogated him, more closely than my own father! Four hours after you met him at the station, he was still talking about your glare.

John: Bosh. That boy wouldn't last ten minutes in question period.

Viv: "Most of your feelings?"

John: Pardon?

Viv: You said you attribute "most of your feelings." I believe, Mr. Brownlee, that that would imply you had other feelings about my engagement.

John: I really don't understand. What is it that you expect, Miss—Mrs.—

Viv: I guess I want a few more glimpses behind that curtain of starchy rectitude. When the curtain parts, I see someone warm, and funny, generous, and just a bit daft. And I like him, John.

John: Not as much as you liked Caldwell.

Viv: John—

John: My own eyes, Vivian. We came to pick you up at the station, but Johnny was already there. I had no desire to get in the way of two young people in love.

Viv: Oh, John. For such an intelligent man—

John: I beg your—

Viv: It was never love, all right? Johnny was kind, and rather sweet.

John snorts.

Viv: And he wasn't already married.

Scene 14

April 1933. Vivian enters John's office and closes the door behind her. John is initially oblivious to her attitude as he signs papers at his desk.

John: Ah, Vivian. I just have some orders-in-council to sign, and we can head to my house for dinner.

Viv: That's fine.

John: Your day was productive?

Viv: It was all right. Gladys told me about this one divorce case she was typing up. Very saucy.

As she talks about the story, he is sucked in despite himself.

John: These are confidential files, I assume.

Viv: Well, if you can't trust the premier . . . Anyway, this one woman in Calgary filed for divorce after receiving a letter from an old friend in Edmonton. The friend heard that the woman's husband was up for a visit, and that he and his wife were staying at the Selkirk Hotel. Well, the friend dropped by the Selkirk Hotel. She found the husband in a dressing gown, smoking and drinking with another woman.

A transcript of the friend's letter was with the file. The letter was just the most perfect blend of innuendo, moral outrage, and—what was it you called it once? When the Liberal leader tripped and slid under his desk in the house? That German word.

John: Schadenfreude.

Viv: Schadenfreude. This old friend writing to tell a woman about her husband's infidelity. Hating the cheating husband. Speaking so lovingly to the wife . . . but tearing her life to shreds. Then she goes on in the letter to discuss her children's school activities.

John returns to signing.

John: Well, take comfort that you've got some time before you need to worry about such matrimonial tribulations.

Viv: Have you decided yet when you're taking your vacation this summer? I'm still rather the junior girl, and if I want to have any chance of taking them with you—with the family—then I should probably be getting my requests in sharply. But I'm so looking forward to a week or two away. I thought it would be terrific to—

John: Vivian, of course you're welcome to join us. We're contemplating a trip to Ontario in July. Coincides with my work on the Banking Commission. But I'd assumed that you'd want to spend your vacation with the Caldwell boy. After his exams—

Viv: He proposed.

John: I see. And you've—

Viv: I've put him off. For now.

John: Well, that's . . . Congratulations.

Viv: I haven't said yes yet.

John: Yes. Well, but he has reasonable prospects. Medical school. And he seems to make you, well, to make you—

Viv: I wanted to talk to you first.

He rises. They end up quite close together.

John: Well, that's very wise.

Viv: Of course, it would change everything. I'd have to leave off working soon. Starting to set my own little table, not coming over to help Mrs. Brownlee.

John: Well, and the boys would certainly miss you.

Viv: And I'd miss them! And I'd miss you.

John: Well, I'd miss our discussions as well. You have a remarkably mature understanding for a girl your age.

Viv: A girl who's a woman, about to turn twenty-two.

John: Quite. Practically an old maid.

Viv: Ancient.

They kiss, briefly. A break. More kissing, longer this time.

Viv: You're pretty good at that.

John: You show considerable talent yourself.

Viv: For an old maid.

More kissing. Not as long.

John: This is madness.

Viv: Yes.

John: I'll just lock the door, then.

He does so. An especially passionate kiss. They step into 1937.

Scene 15

Viv: It was a good week, as I recall.

John: Nine days. Nine very fine days.

Viv: And then.

John: Yes.

They are in the car. She is beaming, he is fidgety.

Viv: *So* delicious to sit with everyone at dinner, and to feel like there's a secret that only the two of us share. Mmm. The new Studebaker is a dream.

John: It's a sound purchase for the government. The motoring literature assured me that the Studebaker Dictator is very reliable. Gets as much as twenty-five miles to the gallon! Large enough to conduct meetings in the back.

Viv: *Pointing.* What's that?

John: Oh, some German outfit has managed to find a way to shrink a Radiola down to fit into an auto. A Motorola, they're called. They use the battery—

Vivian turns a switch. Music blares out—Fats Waller's "How Can You Face Me."

Viv: Ooh! I love this song.

Vivian begins singing along. John pulls the car over and watches her.

> How can you face me
> After what I've gone through
> All on account of you
> Tearin' my heart in two?
> Have you no conscience?
> How could you be so bold?
> Why have you grown so cold?
> After the lies you told?
> No one now seems to be on the level.
> Since I found that—

John turns off the radio.

John: Best to be conserving the battery.

Viv: I was thinking . . . I know Miss Brown has been your personal secretary forever.

John: Since I started practicing law.

Viv: *But* I was thinking that, with all of the work you do out of town, perhaps you need a travelling secretary. Someone to keep track of your appointments, update your agendas . . . take shorthand at those meetings in the car.

John: I'll give you shorthand.

He lunges across the seat, tickling her. She inadvertently hurts him.

John: Ow!

Viv: Oh! Are you all right?

John: Right as rain. Perhaps we could adjourn to the back seat?

Viv: Where are we?

John: Well, either on the second service road south of Stony Plain, or exactly in the middle of nowhere.

They shift to the back seat. Lights fade to black.

Viv: Shall I?

John: Oh, yes please. *Pause.* Not that! Ow.

Viv: Sorry. Ow.

John: That was you?

Viv: I'll lift my leg up.

John: Uh!

Viv: Well, perhaps if you shift your—

John: Ah. Yes. That seems to be—

Viv: Mmm.

John: MMMMmmm.

Lights up. He is zipping his fly. She is checking her makeup.

Viv: So you'll think about it?

John: About?

Viv: Me as your travelling secretary. To go with you when you go off for speeches, meetings in Calgary. Or if you end up going back to Europe—

John: I'm not certain that's a good idea, Vivian. I should get you back.

They move back to the front seat.

Viv: How long do you think we can keep this up—slipping away while you're at a "meeting." Trading glances when Florence is away from the dinner table.

John: Please! We've got to be careful. You know that Florence isn't . . . strong. Any word of this . . . it would kill her.

Viv: Yes, I'm certain it's Florence you're thinking about.

Silence.

John: Let's just try to enjoy this for as long as it lasts.

Viv: And how long is that, John? Long enough for you to get your butter churned, and then you drop me like a stone into the river.

John: Now, that's not what I meant. You need to calm yourself, Vivian.

Viv: I *am* calm. What did you think back when we started this?

John: "Back when we started?" It was last week!

Viv: For you, maybe! I've been thinking . . .

John: You've been thinking what? You've been thinking about this for longer? *Pause. A nod.* A lot longer.

Viv: Not all the time. A look, a few kind words. These things accumulate, John. And don't think I didn't see your eyes flick sometimes.

John: My eyes?

Viv: When a gentleman passes by a lady, and the lady is adept, she may gauge a gentleman's true feelings by two things, simply by turning around.

John: Is that so?

Viv: If a gentleman's eyes flick up to meet yours, it is clear that he was admiring your backside. And if he blushes, even a little, it means that he liked what he saw. Honestly, how do men get anything done when they don't know the first thing about anything?

John: Well, I do know that taking you with me on business trips as my travelling secretary is a perfect way to get every tongue in the province wagging.

Viv: You think I want the entire world to think of me as the premier's—

John: That's why it's imperative we be careful. Now, I have a meeting at 3:00 PM on Saturday. I can quietly cancel. Would you be able to stay late at your office—

Viv: This is the way it's going to be, isn't it? This is the rest of my life with you.

John: Vivian, I don't . . . I'm not sure what this will mean after I'm finished with politics. Be patient.

Viv: I still haven't given Johnny an answer, you know. Keep putting him off. I don't even know why. There's no way I can marry him.

John: Well, why not? *Silence.* I mean, if you're so dissatisfied with our situation.

Viv: I suppose that that would be the efficient, the politic thing to do, the way you might handle the situation. Use something up and then move on.

John: Well, we can't very well—

Viv: I'm not like that. I want the man who danced with me on that muddy July night in Edson. I want the man who bullies me into learning shorthand, and makes me laugh, and listens to what I have to say about politics. Or pretends to listen.

John: I don't pretend.

Viv: But that's never going to happen, is it? This will never be anything but the briefest of flings. Never acknowledged and soon discarded for safety's sake.

John: I made you no promises, Vivian. I was very careful.

Viv: Oh, I have no doubt about that. Your whole life. Careful. Oh, God. I've got to get clear of this. Clear of you. Let me out.

John: Don't be foolish, Vivian.

Viv: I . . . I feel ill.

John: We're not far to your home now. Can you—

She can't. He pulls over. She piles out; standing as she retches. He clambers out and comforts her awkwardly. He is very aware this is a public street back in town.

John: There. There. There. Better?

Viv: A little bit.

John: You'll see this so differently in the morning light, Vivian. You'll see. There's such a wide world out in front of you.

Viv: John, you're not dying. You're throwing me out.

John: I'm not! I'd be happy to continue . . . to continue as we are. You're thoughtful. You're intelligent. And you have the capacity to be discreet.

Viv: You sound like you're listing my qualifications to be a page in the legislature. Not your—what am I, John?

John: I . . . I have no name for this, Vivian.

Viv: At least now I can tell Johnny why I can't marry him.

John: Tell him? That's utterly foolish, Vivian.

Viv: Who knows? He might even forgive—

He grabs her. They struggle.

John: Don't be stupid, girl. No one can ever know. Perhaps I can even help the two of you. A young couple, starting out in life. A little boost.

Viv: Let me go, John!

John: Telling Caldwell would be the first step down a very bad path, Vivian. Very bad—for both of us.

Viv: You're hurting—

Scene 16

He releases her. She takes a step away. A silence. Shift back to 1937.

John: If only you had kept quiet.

Viv: God damn you.

She exits. He slips into reverie. Becomes a radio address.

John: I have just formally tendered my resignation to his honour the lieutenant-governor, and requested him to call upon Gordon Reid to form a government. Mr. Reid has been one of the most faithful of my ministers. I have every confidence in his ability and judgment. I leave the service of the province after thirteen years with a clear conscience that during that time I have given the best I have in the interests of the people.

Vivian returns with a copy of the judgment.

Viv: The verdict. Split decision, if it's any consolation. Six to three. "Judgment should be entered in favour of the appellant Vivian Sorenson against the respondent John Brownlee for the sum of ten thousand dollars. And this court does further order that the respondent Brownlee pay the appellant Sorenson the costs incurred by the said appellant—"

John: Impossible!

Viv: It's done, now. I finally got what the jury said—

John: There's precedent—

Viv: It's over, John. I told a better story.

John: It's not over. I'm prepared to put in a special request to appeal to the Privy Council of the British Empire.

Viv: What does it matter, John? You've lost. We've . . . lost.

John: Vivian?

She exits.

End

ACKNOWLEDGMENTS

The inaugural productions of all four of these plays were sponsored by the Provincial Archives of Alberta. We are deeply indebted to the outstanding support of that organization and its staff and volunteers. This book has been made possible by the support of the Friends of the Provincial Archives of Alberta Society, and we wish to express our deep gratitude.

The following were instrumental in the development of these plays: Pamela Anthony, Andrea Beca, Tony Cashman, Jason Chatterley, Trish Chatterley, the Edmonton Arts Council, the Edmonton Heritage Council, the Edmonton Public Library, Franklin Foster, Anna Gibson-Hollow, Rose Ginther, Grant MacEwan University, Leslie Hall, Ian Jackson, Irene Jendzjowsky, Jessica King, Myrna Kostash, Leslie Latta Guthrie, LitFest: Edmonton's Nonfiction Festival, Gina Moe, Nicole Moeller, Bradley Moss, Mary Lou Ng, Tammy O'Handley, One Yellow Rabbit, Jill Roszell, Gayle Simonson, Rosalind Smith, Jan Taylor, and Linda Wood Edwards.

We are especially indebted to the actors and designers who have brought their own genius and craft to these plays: Mark Anderako, Paul Bezaire, Randy Brososky, Nicole Diebert, Geri Dittrich, Jenny McKillop, Steve Pirot, Gina Puntil, Kirsten Rasmussen, and Heather D. Swain.

Debbie Marshall is grateful for the love, friendship, and support provided by Monica Newton, the daughter of Beatrice Nasmyth. Monica preserved her mother's wartime letters and generously shared them with Debbie. Sadly, Monica passed away in April 2012. *Firing Lines* is dedicated to her memory.

Debbie also acknowledges the assistance of Bernie Quigley, a descendant of Fred Sutton, a soldier featured in her play. She also appreciated the help of the WWI-L listserv, a group of researchers, scholars, and historians who provided helpful answers to many of her war-related queries. Finally, she is thankful for the unflagging support of her family: Heather Marshall, Jonathan and Amanda Morgan, and Rachel Culbertson.

For information on performance rights of all of these plays, please contact MAA and PAA Theatre, cheoros@hotmail.com, 780.479.2795.

DAVID CHEOROS has produced festivals and events for more than twenty years, including five years as festival director of the Edmonton Fringe Theatre Festival. He is the producer of LitFest: Edmonton's Nonfiction Festival, and teaches at Grant MacEwan University. David has toured his own productions across North America and to Australia, and has produced and directed half a dozen short films. He and Karen Simonson are the founders of MAA and PAA Theatre. Please visit www.maapaa.ca.

KAREN SIMONSON is a reference archivist at the Provincial Archives of Alberta. She was born and raised in Edmonton, and has a BA (Hons) in history from the University of Alberta and an MA in archival studies from the University of Manitoba. In 2006, Karen and David Cheoros co-founded the MAA and PAA Theatre, which is dedicated to the use of primary sources to tell original stories in a contemporary and engaging manner. Please visit www.maapaa.ca.

DEBBIE MARSHALL is a writer, editor, and playwright. She is the author of *Give Your Other Vote to the Sister: A Woman's Journey into the Great War*, the story of Roberta MacAdams, a First World War nurse and politician. Her play *Firing Lines* is based on the Great War writings of foreign correspondent Beatrice Nasmyth and was produced in conjunction with the Provincial Archives of Alberta in August 2012 at the Edmonton Fringe Festival. Debbie also writes a monthly blog that features Canadian nurses who died during the First World War. To learn more, please visit www.rememberingfirstworldwarnurses. blogspot.ca.